THE COMPLETE GUIDE TO BUYING A SECOND HOME OR REAL ESTATE IN MEXICO

Insider Secrets You Need to Know

By Jackie Bondanza

THE COMPLETE GUIDE TO BUYING A SECOND HOME OR REAL ESTATE IN MEXICO: INSIDER SECRETS YOU NEED TO KNOW

1405 SW 6th Avenue • Ocala, Florida 34471 • Phone **352-622-1825** • Fax 352-622-1875 Web site: www.atlantic-pub.com • E-mail: sales@atlantic-pub.com SANNumber:268-1250

Library of Congress Cataloging-in-Publication Data

Bondanza, Jackie, 1980-
 The complete guide to buying a second home or real estate in Mexico : insider secrets you need to know / by Jackie Bondanza.
    p. cm.
 Includes bibliographical references and index.
 ISBN-13: 978-1-60138-131-6 (alk. paper)
 ISBN-10: 1-60138-131-X (alk. paper)
 1. Real estate investment--Mexico. 2. Second homes--Mexico. 3. House buying--Mexico. I. Title.
 HD328.B66 2009
 643'.120972--dc22
                        2009036890

Printed in the United States

PROJECT MANAGER: Erin Everhart • eeverhart@atlantic-pub.com
INTERIOR DESIGN: Antoinette D'Amore • addesign@videotron.ca
ASSISTANT EDITOR: Angela Pham • apham@atlantic-pub.com
COVER AND JACKET DESIGN: Jackie Miller • sullmill@charter.net

Over the years, we have adopted a number of dogs from rescues and shelters. First there was Bear and after he passed, Ginger and Scout. Now, we have Kira, another rescue. They have brought immense joy and love not just into our lives, but into the lives of all who met them.

We want you to know a portion of the profits of this book will be donated in Bear, Ginger and Scout's memory to local animal shelters, parks, conservation organizations, and other individuals and nonprofit organizations in need of assistance.

– Douglas & Sherri Brown,
President & Vice-President of Atlantic Publishing

ACKNOWLEDGEMENTS

There are a number of people to whom I am indebted for their valuable insight and guidance on purchasing real estate in Mexico. Thanks to Wayne Franklin of Tropicasa Realty, Chris Snell of Snell Real Estate, Mauricio Rojas, Brad Grieve, Murphy O'Brien Public Relations, and all the case study participants.

I would like to especially thank the "A" team: Linda Neil of The Settlement Company, Bruce Greenberg of Montaña Verde, and Matthew A. Miller of ConfiCasa Mortgage International for their time, professional guidance, and genuine enthusiasm throughout the writing process. Without them, this book would not have been possible. This is dedicated to them.

I would also like to thank Atlantic Publishing Group and my lovely and talented editor Erin Everhart for her dedicated and professional support and patience.

Lastly, I would like to thank James, Allie, and Eileen for their continued love and support.

TABLE OF CONTENTS

Chapter 3: How to Decide if Buying is Right For You   65

PART II: Beginning Your Search   79

Chapter 4: Top 15 Mexican Real Estate Markets   81

Chapter 5: What to Look Out For and What to Avoid   121

PART III: The Process of Purchasing, Financing, and Securing Your Investment 215

Chapter 9: The Process of Purchasing 217

Chapter 10: Financing Your Investment 249

FOREWORD

The first time I bought real estate internationally was on the southwest coast of Nicaragua on the outskirts of a small town called El Ostional. In order to understand the property line, my realtor, a knowledgeable local land owner, the farmer of the land, and I took out a machete and cut our way through overgrown grass to the property. There was no survey done; I could not even tell how big the parcel was. I was not even sure that this farmer was the owner of the property. There were no rules, no process, and lots of risk. We agreed on the numbers on the spot, half the time speaking in Spanish and half in English. I sent my first deposit check directly to the realtor. I took a huge risk, and I cannot say that the purchase was hassle-free. Many years later, I am still dealing with property line and easement issues that were not disclosed during the purchase. Regardless, I am satisfied with my investment.

The property had panoramic views of the ocean and the coastline and was just a few minutes from a deserted, white sandy beach. It was situated on the Costa Rican border, where real estate values had skyrocketed in previous years. In my mind, this area had tremendous potential. A main coastal highway was being planned for the west, and the town 20 miles to the north was growing leaps and bounds. I knew I wanted to get in this market; I just did not know how. There was no formula, guide, or established process to acquire the land; I just winged it. I had bought real estate many times before in the United States and have always been a firm believer in a diversified portfolio with a heavier investment in real estate over stocks. I knew that oceanfront and ocean view property was never going be attainable for me on U.S. soil, so I had to look abroad. I also understood that there was only so much land like this to be purchased. I wanted to get in early, and I am glad I did. The property has increased in value by about 10 percent, and the area has become more popular over time.

There are many variables that afford us the opportunity to go south of the border to look for vacation and retirement homes or investment properties. Land values have increased significantly in the past two decades despite some temporary downturns. For someone looking to live the good life — on a beach, in warm weather, or on the golf course — doing so in the U.S. may not be an option because of high prices. Just one look at real estate in Mexico, and you will be amazed at what value you get for the money. The retirement lifestyle you dreamed of can truly be a reality because of the affordability, beauty, and ease of life that Mexico provides.

Before the Internet age, living abroad — so far from your family and friends, and out of communication — seemed like a far-fetched idea. Given the ubiquity of the Internet, e-mail, cell phones, and video chat, we can live nearly anywhere in the world and still be in touch with our loved ones. This makes retiring or living aboard much more manageable. You can be living the good life, with a margarita in one hand, knowing that you are still in touch and reachable in case of emergency.

Plus, there is the fear of the unknown. Searching, investigating, and investing one's life savings to buy real estate in another country can be scary. The thought can be daunting, even for the most savvy real estate investors.

Would I ever advise someone to take the path that I took in Nicaragua? The answer is, flat-out, no. You need to have a guide —

like this book — written by experienced professionals. Purchasing real estate is one of the most expensive transactions most people will ever make in their lifetime. Even in the U.S., the process is complicated, requires a lot of thought, and can be a very stressful, emotional time for many buyers. You should never go at it alone. But in the U.S., we are lucky enough to have long established rules and laws that govern the process. There are entire industries and thousands of businesses that were created to protect buyers, sellers, and everyone else involved in the transaction.

As more foreigners are buying land in Mexico, the process is becoming more refined. The government and the businesses that benefit from real estate and tourism are helping ameliorate the process. *The Complete Guide to Buying a Second Home or Real Estate in Mexico* is truly the bible for anyone considering getting into the international real estate market. It is an easy-to-read guide and includes informative case studies from people who have pounded the pavement and learned the hard lessons already; they have not only researched the process, but the important players and laws involved every step of the way. Written in a very informative and descriptive way, this book covers the nuts and bolts of buying real estate in Mexico. Based on my experience, it has not missed a beat. It is well laid-out and highlights all the important considerations before you even get on an airplane to visit. The book is an honest look at how things are done in Mexico; it tells you how to adjust your mindset to the new processes and culture. The author clearly outlines where the hurdles are, what to look out for, and where to spend extra time on research and discovery. You can literally carry this book with you as you go through the process.

The Complete Guide to Buying a Second Home or Real Estate in Mexico is not a sales book on buying land in Mexico, but an honest guide covering everything you would ever need to know. It starts with a high-level description of the types of real estate you can buy in Mexico and the advantages of each. Then, it takes you through each step of the purchase process. The book takes you through many parts of the country and educates you on the real estate markets, investment opportunities, upsides, and downsides. With real-life anecdotes scattered throughout the book and quotes from real people doing business in the country, you can be confident that this book is the guide that you need.

Anyone who has ever thought about or even a dreamed about buying real estate in Mexico should pick up *The Complete Guide to Buying a Second Home or Real Estate in Mexico*. Use it as a reference guide every step of the way.

Brendon DeSimone,
Real Estate Expert, Paragon Real Estate Group

Brendon DeSimone is a successful entrepreneur, real estate investor, and businessman who has leveraged his expertise to become a leading residential real estate expert.

DeSimone is regularly featured on Home and Garden Television's (HGTV) "Curb Appeal," "National Open House," "Bank For Your Buck," and "My House is Worth What?" When reporting on breaking real estate news, reporters at leading San Francisco Bay Area television news programs, as well as national print publications, frequently seek DeSimone's expertise and savvy market perspective.

*DeSimone has transacted more than $100 million in sales. He owns and manages real estate in three states, as well as in Latin America. He started at a Silicon Valley Internet start-up in business development and helped grow the company significantly before he turned his attention and developed business sense to real estate. DeSimone has a proven track record of helping clients get maximum value from the purchase or sale of a residential property. Learn more at **www.brendondesimone.com**.*

INTRODUCTION

With sprawling, white sandy beaches and sparkling blue waters; the tiny villages flavored with zesty authenticity and European flare; and clusters of mountains dotted with lush tropical forests, Mexico is a land of rich culture and admirable beauty. It comes as little surprise, then, that more than one million Americans call Mexico home these days — at least for part of the year. Whether it is for the beautiful serenity of the country's beaches or for the affordable and relaxed lifestyle, foreigners are increasingly turning to Mexico to retire, relocate, and get some plain old R&R.

Over the past 15 to 20 years, the nature and direction of both the Mexican tourism and real estate business have shifted dramatically. Twenty years ago, Americans were not as inclined to invest in real estate in Mexico, as the process was — for lack of a better phrase — quite questionable. The Mexican government had little involvement in the process, and there were few laws to protect foreigners' investments. The lack of regulation, coupled with the unclear and often complicated process of purchasing property, have drained countless people of their life savings and perpetuated the inaccurate idea that purchasing real estate in Mexico was a less than a smart investment.

However, as Mexican citizens began to fully realize the potential of their undeveloped land, the government began reforming and amending laws and regulations that allowed foreigners to purchase real estate in Mexico much more easily. In Mexico today, real estate agents, attorneys, and banks are increasingly conscientious, and investors are much more protected and well-informed. The process of investing in real estate is similar to the process that exists in the United States and other developed countries, which has led to a tremendous boom over the past decade in investors purchasing property on Mexico's beautiful beaches. The purchasing trend is expected to continue to increase at a rapid pace in the future as an explosion of interested investors from the U.S., Canada, and Europe purchase property in Mexico.

The draw to Mexico has existed for decades but has become a realistic opportunity for many more recently, thanks to a collaborative effort by the Mexican government and Mexican and American banks, mortgage companies, real estate agents, and sellers alike. As purchasing real estate in Mexico has become more accessible, realistic, and logical, the process has made significant headway in the past six to 12 months. As demand for across-the-border financing has increased, mortgage companies have established more opportunities for investors to access financing for purchasing property in Mexico. In the past, getting a bank to finance a mortgage for property in a foreign country was difficult, to say the least. Today there exists a variety of secure financing options for your Mexican getaway that open the doors of opportunity for more potential investors than ever before.

As far as the Mexican real estate industry has come, a little caution still goes a long way. Investors need to remain informed and prepared when considering purchasing property in Mexico, as the process involves plenty of legal formalities, time, and research. Horror stories about investors being swindled out of their life savings have created a misconception that purchasing real estate in Mexico is a sure-fire way to lose your hard-earned money. In 2000, a story unfolded about the Baja Beach and Tennis Club in Punta Banda, where nearly 200 American and other foreign investors were forced out of their homes because of a dispute over the land. Because the developer built on land that was being disputed in the Mexican court and somehow convinced investors to purchase in his development while the nature of the land was being disputed, his investors inevitably lost millions when the government ultimately ruled that the land was protected and the developer should have never built on it. Not only did investors lose millions, but the developer also ruined protected agriculture, sand dunes, and wetlands.

More recently, the Trump Ocean Resort in Baja met a similar fate. Investors, fed with promises of a luxurious, five-star, oceanfront high-rise condominium, plunked down more than $30 million for units in the project before any concrete had even been poured. When the developer, who licensed Trump's name for the project, ran out of money as the U.S. crashed in 2008, investors were left with little more than building supplies.

Stories like these should serve as cautionary tales of what *not* to do when investing in Mexican real estate and should emphasize just how important it is to follow each step in the purchasing process, like obtaining the land deed, doing a title search, confirming the seller has the right to sell, determining if a developer has obtained proper clearance to develop land, and consulting with the Ministry of Foreign Relations to determine your property use. When investors are armed with the proper knowledge of the process and an understanding of and respect for the legal requirements, purchasing real estate in Mexico is a fun, exciting, and profitable experience.

Although the government has cleaned up the real estate industry significantly since the 1990s and prior when there was an "anything goes" attitude, there undoubtedly still exist "professionals" in the industry in Mexico who attempt to convince investors otherwise. There also remain investors who do not follow the rules in hopes of cutting corners for time or money reasons — and who end up with nothing in the end. This book aims to outline the avenues to avoiding situations like these and how to be a smart investor.

The Complete Guide to Buying a Second Home or Real Estate in Mexico is an easy-to-read guide that breaks down each step in the purchasing process and provides the crucial information every investor needs to know before purchasing Mexican property. In addition to providing essential information about investing, this book also discusses all the things that come along with buying real estate in a foreign country, including the cost of heating and cooling your home; what kind of taxes you can expect to pay; the process of establishing residency; how to obtain medical care; how to set a budget and determine a down payment; how to make moving plans; and how to get around. Here, you will also find information and insider tips from some of the top real estate agents, closing agents, mortgage brokers, and other professionals in the industry — as well as personal stories of people who have actually gone through the process of buying a home in Mexico.

Divided into four parts, *The Complete Guide to Buying a Second Home or Real Estate in Mexico* takes you through the process of investing as it would realistically unfold. Part I discusses how to determine if buying is even right for you and explains the basics of the Mexican legal system, the different types of property available, and the investment process in Mexico. Part II takes you through the beginning of your search and details how to find a trustworthy real estate agent, attorney, and bank; what you should look for when choosing a property; the pros and cons of buying versus building; and when to consider renting your property. Part II also presents the top locations around the country that provide the best deals for your money, as well as what to look out for and what to avoid.

Once you have determined the type of property to invest in, you will need to know what you can expect from your time and money. Part III focuses on this part of the process and details planning your home buying timeline; negotiating a great deal; determining your down payment; understanding the contracts; how to get a property appraisal; and what you can expect when closing the deal. The chapters in this part also explain how to do a legal title search, how to determine if the seller has the right to sell (and if your property will need to be held in a trust), the smartest way to finance your investment, and the option of using your current home equity or your IRA to finance your second home.

In addition to being knowledgeable about the legal terms and details of the real estate process, you should also know a little bit about the ins and outs of living in Mexico if you are considering purchasing property there. Part IV discusses Mexican living, the geography and climate, safety, transportation, medical care, and what you can expect when living in a foreign country. This book also includes an Appendix of key real estate and legal terms for your reference. After all, the best way to approach this process is with a firm understanding of what to expect, as well as all the help and insider information available to you.

Despite the surge of negative attention that Mexico has received lately — particularly in U.S. media — the country remains a thriving, safe, profitable, and beautiful place. Just like in any country, pockets of crime and poverty exist, and potential buyers should approach an investment with knowledge, logic, and information. As Mexico struggles to regulate the drug cartels that exist within its borders, the country also continues to grow economically. According to a February 2009 article in *The Wall Street Journal*, despite the increased attention and concern surrounding the drug cartels, Mexico's economy remains one of the Top 20 strongest economies in the world. Sociologically, the country's poverty levels continue to decrease.

Despite the often-volatile real estate market throughout the United States and other parts of the world, the Mexican real estate market continues to grow steadily and there is no greater time than now to invest. There is something for everyone in Mexico, and *The Complete Guide to Buying a Second Home or Real Estate in Mexico* aims to provide the direction and information to guide future investors to their dream homes in Mexico's tropical paradise. Happy reading, and more importantly, smart investing.

PART I

What You Should Know Before You Buy

CHAPTER 1

The Kinds of Properties
to Consider

Although most people think of beaches and tropical weather when they think of Mexico, the country offers a diversity of real estate options in a variety of locations — from tiny villages tucked away in the mountains of Central Mexico to busy cities like Guadalajara and Mexico City, which serve as hubs for international travel and business.

For some people, deciding where they want to purchase property is easy. For others who perhaps are not as familiar with Mexico or are interested in a lesser-known area of the country, a little research goes a long way. Considering the variety of property and narrowing down what you are looking for is the first step to purchasing in Mexico, and it is essential to know the differences in the types of property you are looking at, as the type will help determine your purchasing steps and define the parameters of the property use. Generally, Mexican property is defined as private, public, or social (like *ejidal* land). Private property can be categorized as either residential, industrial, or commercial.

First, it is important to understand *ejidal* land and the restricted zone before you begin your search.

Ejidal Land

Ejidal land is government land that is in possession of a large group of people, usually those in extended families or a small community. The Mexican Constitution, specifically agrarian law, governs and outlines the specifications and parameters of the *ejidal* land. The purpose of creating this category of land was to distribute it to Mexican nationals as part of the process of establishing a country and to encourage distribution of land to classes of people who otherwise might not have been able to afford it. The *ejidal* concept was developed as a result of the Mexican revolution of 1917. Peasants, known as *ejidatarios* once they became part of the *ejido*, could petition to become part of an *ejido* community. According to Linda Neil of The Settlement Company®, as of 1992, *ejidal* lands represented nearly half the land in the country. "Communal land, which represents other land surrounding the indigenous villages, were established in pre-Hispanic times and are not generally offered for sale," she said. Neil is founder of The Settlement Company, a consultancy firm that specializes in closing and escrow services, title transfer, and insurance for Mexican real estate purchases.

Because of the regulations outlined in Mexico's constitution, there were few opportunities for foreigners to buy land or real estate in the country for many years until 1992, when the government allowed *ejidatarios* to convert their land to private property and sell it.

Can I Buy *Ejidal* Land?

Yes, but it is not necessarily easy. As will be discussed in Chapter 2, amendments to the agrarian law granted the *ejidatarios* the right to convert their portion of the *ejido* to private property and then sell it.

Investors may purchase individual parcels of *ejidal* land or have rights to the *ejido*'s common land. Many larger developers have had success in acquiring the property that can be privatized within an *ejido*. Today, there are many legal developments in popular vacation and second home areas, including Guadalajara, Los Cabos, and Puerto Vallarta. However, investors should be wary of developers who do not have the proper documents. It is always recommended that potential buyers research the property — either through a company, attorney, or other professional who specializes in *ejidal* matters — to ensure the developer does indeed have the title to the land and that the process of converting the land has been completed. Otherwise, there exists potential for disaster, much like the experience of the investors at the Baja Beach and Tennis Club in Ensenada who lost their homes and millions of dollars because the developer never disclosed that the land was being disputed.

The Process of Privatization

While foreigners are now able to purchase this once-restricted land that is valuable real estate in some of the country's best locations, the process of purchasing *ejidal* land is very involved and requires a significant amount of time, research, and patience. In a nutshell, the *ejido* board (called the *Asamblea de Ejidatarios*) must agree to privatize certain portions of the *ejidal* territory and agree to grant individual ownership rights to an *ejidatario*, then the *ejidatario* wishing to sell the land must apply to have the land removed as *ejidal* property. Once that is granted, the individual can then sell the land because it is not part of the *ejido* anymore, and transfer the title to a new investor.

Once an *ejidatario* decides to sell his or her property, the investor is required to make an offer in writing, which is then presented to the rest of the members of the *ejido*, who vote to approve or reject the offer. If the offer is accepted, it will remain with the *ejido* for 30 days, during which time any member of the *ejido* is eligible to buy the property by matching the investor's offer. Should the 30 days pass and no *ejidatario* has expressed interest in purchasing the property, the investor may purchase it at that point. A document that certifies that the procedure has been followed is essential; this will ensure the process is complete and valid.

Before an *ejidal* property can even be considered for sale, the Mexican government must appraise the property and determine its boundaries. The *comisario*, or the president of the *ejido*, determines if the property is approved for sale, and the sale must then be approved by and documented in the *Reforma Agraria* (Agrarian Reform). After this process, the *ejidatario* can initiate the process of selling his or her parcel of land. Only after all of these steps have been successfully completed will the *ejidatario* be granted the deed to the land and be able to sell the land and transfer the deed to a foreigner.

So is purchasing *ejido* property even worth it? Yes, if you follow the proper steps, comprehend and respect the legal process, and understand that the process will be a time-consuming one. Because so much valuable property in Mexico is *ejidal* land, the government is working to make the process of privatizing the land easier so more foreigners can purchase it.

You should never purchase *ejidal* land that has not been fully privatized or that is in the process of being privatized. The process of privatizing can take years, thus involving yourself in an investment in a piece of property that has not gone through the process is not a wise choice. You should discontinue your relationship with any realtor or professional who tells you otherwise, as they probably do not have your best interests in mind.

The Restricted Zone

Mexico's restricted zone, also referred to as the prohibited zone, comprises any property located within roughly 30 miles of any coastline (which, naturally, includes beachfront property), and within 60 miles of any Mexican border. More than a century ago, the restricted zone was initially created to protect valuable land from foreign invaders; it was never meant as a deterrent to foreign investors. Seeing the inherent value of property in the restricted zone, and realizing the need for foreign investment, the government permitted the acquisition of residential properties by foreigners through the use of the *fideicomiso* in 1973. The Foreign Investment Act, as a part of the NAFTA trade agreement between the U.S. and Mexico, outlined additional guidelines and modifications to the process in the 1990s.

Given the geography of the country, a significant part of valuable land falls within the restricted zone. Because so much valuable real estate falls into this category, the government began easing restrictions a few decades ago as it recognized the value of the property in the zone. For example, the entire Baja Peninsula is located within the restricted zone. Now, foreign buyers can purchase property and enjoy property rights in the restricted zone through the use of a bank trust.

The *Fideicomiso*

The *fideicomiso* is a trust that must be set up with a Mexican bank in order to purchase residential property in the restricted zone. The bank acts as your trustee to the land, which you are then free to use as your own. When you want to sell the land, the trust is transferred to the new buyer. If you are buying a piece of property that is already in a bank trust, the trust is simply transferred to you as the new buyer. If you sell your property, the Ministry of Foreign Affairs must be notified of the change in ownership. The bank will most likely handle this notification for you. Although foreign buyers do not technically own the land on a restricted zone property, they do own the property rights and, therefore, the freedom to live on the land, lease the land, borrow money against the land, and make modifications and improvements to it.

According to the document "Purchasing Your Dream Home in Mexico," by Linda Neil, "In practical terms, the beneficiary has full control of the property. He may direct the trustee bank to lease the property, mortgage the property, or sell the property. The foreign owner enjoys full rights of usage and may do anything to the property permitted under Mexican law. He enjoys the same rights of dominion as any Mexican citizen who has direct title to the property. He may construct a building, tear it down, or modify it in compliance only with the local zoning and planning ordinances or, if applicable, the homeowner's condo-minium regime."

If the bank that holds your trust goes bankrupt, the trust will be transferred to another bank, and you will not lose your property. Many of the well-known banks in Mexico act as trustees for *fidei-comisos*. There has been a misconception in the past that Mexican banks are less than trustworthy when it comes to foreigners' money, but the majority of the Mexican banking business is tied to the rest of the world, just like here in the United States. Many of the banks are international, like Deutsche and HSBC, as well as national, like the Banco de México. One of the larger banks — national or international — will probably be the bank you deal with to set up your trust. That does not mean, however, that a smaller Mexican bank should not be trusted. Assuming you do your homework and hire a good closing agent and real estate agent, they will guide you in the right direction when it comes to setting up your trust with a reputable bank.

The Ministry of Foreign Affairs controls all the activity involving a *fideicomiso*, and you will have to apply for a permit through the ministry to do any of the following:

- Establish a trust with a bank for purchase of property in the restricted zone

- Increase the area covered by the trust

- Change the trust in any way, which includes changing the beneficiary or adding one

- Establish a Mexican corporation

If you are looking for a vacation or retirement home, chances are you will be attracted to a development in the restricted zone. In this case, your closing agent or real estate agent should begin the process of applying for a permit from the Ministry of Foreign Affairs, which will then grant you the access to set up a trust with a Mexican bank. In general, you can expect to pay roughly $1,500 to establish your trust, $500 to register it in the National Foreign Investment Registry, and about $500 annually.

To streamline and speed up the process of obtaining the necessary permits, the Mexican government recently established time guidelines for the ministry. If an application for a permit is requested at the ministry's main location in Mexico City, it must grant the permit, provided it meets the requirements, within five days. If the request is made at another location, the request must be granted within one month. If the ministry does not respond within the allotted time period, the permit will be considered granted. The same holds true when you register your property with the ministry. If the ministry does not confirm your property's registration within 15 days, the property can be considered legally registered. These laws work in the buyer's favor and prevent the ministry from holding up your purchase.

Below is a chart depicting the amount of trusts by year the Ministry of Foreign Affairs grants to buyers purchasing property in the restricted zone. As you can see, the amount of trusts granted peaked during 2005-2007, which is likely a result of the real estate boom in the United States. Because more people were able to get mortgages, the housing market boomed, and more people sought out Mexico for vacation and retirement homes. Undoubtedly, the drop in 2008 can be attributed at least in part to the real estate and financial market crash. Without unlimited access to cash, second and reverse mortgages, home equity loans, and IRA financing, Americans in particular contributed to the decrease in the amount of property bought in Mexico and, ultimately, the amount of trusts granted.

Trusts Granted from the Ministry of Foreign Affairs for Property in the Restricted Zone by Year

2000	2001	2002	2003	2004	2005	2006	2007	2008
1,970	2,033	1,907	2,614	3,720	5,753	6,611	7,000	5,226

Purchasing in the restricted zone is a straightforward process that, given you follow the proper steps, will undoubtedly serve you well in terms of enjoying the property's use and benefiting from its sale (should you decide) in the future. Given the draw to property in the restricted zone and the fast pace at which the Mexican real estate market is growing, you are almost guaranteed a profit when you sell. Of course, you can expect to pay higher prices for restricted zone property up front, but you will ultimately benefit from the profit you will realize when you sell. Much of the property in the restricted zone is in high demand in Mexico — or will be in the near future in up-and-coming areas — so the higher cost you will pay for property will be offset by the profit you make when you sell it.

Forming a Mexican Corporation

The second option for purchasing property in the restricted zone is forming a corporation to use your property for commercial purposes. The Mexican government eased restrictions on commercial property in 1993 when they introduced the Foreign Investment Law, and many entrepreneurs and business owners have taken advantage of the ease in opening bed and breakfasts, retail stores, restaurants, and bars in some of Mexico's most beautiful locations.

So how and why would you form a corporation to buy property? For instance, if you and a business partner who were both American citizens wanted to open a bed and breakfast in Baja, you would be able to purchase property directly without creating a bank trust. Your transaction would be considered "fee simple," meaning you were purchasing property for commercial use and therefore would not need a trust with a bank. A fee simple purchase also includes a residential purchase outside of the restricted zone, where a bank trust is not required.

As seen in this scenario, you do not have to be a Mexican national to be part of an existing corporation. The corporation can be completely foreign-owned and you can establish your corporation in Mexico before you purchase land. Prior to the Foreign Investment Law, your corporation had to be 51 percent owned by Mexican nationals. Because that restriction required foreign businesses and corporations to have majority ownership by Mexicans, it greatly restricted the amount of foreign-owned businesses in the restricted zone. With the new law, it is much easier for retirees and general investors alike to bring their businesses to Mexico.

Buying Property Through Your Mexican Corporation

Forming a corporation in Mexico is a considerably involved process, but it continues to become easier. Typically, it can take up to two months to file all the correct paperwork and obtain the necessary permits to form your corporation. Forming a corporation also allows you to purchase multiple properties, all of which your corporation owns.

To give you a general idea of what you will need to legally form a corporation and purchase property through this corporation, you will need at least the following:

- Two shareholders, who can both be of foreign descent

- An initial investment of 50,000 pesos (about $3,800)

- An accounting system to report your financial activity each month

To establish your Mexican corporation, you must apply to have the name of your corporation recognized to the *Secretaría de Relaciones Exteriores*, the Secretary of Exterior Relations. After you receive approval, you have to sign a variety of documents before a *notario publico* (notary public) for your corporation to be legally recognized. You are then obligated to list your corporation with the National Registry of Foreign Investment, along with the Business and Commerce Registry. You will also have to obtain a visa (most likely an FM3 visa) for any members of the corporation who are foreigners so that they may conduct business in Mexico through the corporation. These steps ensure your corporation is legal.

Similar to the requirements for purchasing unimproved land, if you purchase raw land with no development that is larger than 1,995 square meters (about 20,000 square feet), you will be required to develop on the land and invest a certain amount of money in your construction within one to three years of purchase. Again, this is to avoid empty lots sitting on valuable property and to encourage development and new businesses. This is an important aspect to understand when you are budgeting for your purchase, as you will have to consider that within a short time, you will be required to invest money in your property in order to comply with the conditions of your permit with the Ministry of Foreign Relations. There exists the option of filing a "dormancy election," essentially declaring your corporation dormant, which allows you to put development on hold. Linda Neil advises against this, however, because it is a hassle. To avoid electing dormancy, follow the compliance guidelines and develop within the timeframe of these guidelines when you purchase the property.

Paying taxes on your Mexican corporation can be involved, particularly considering that you may be required to pay both Mexican and American tax, assuming you are a U.S. citizen forming a corporation in Mexico. If you own more than 10 percent of your Mexican corporation, the IRS requires you to file your financial activity and income on your yearly tax returns.

As for Mexican taxes, you will be subject to value-added tax and an acquisition tax when you purchase property, as well as capital gains taxes if you sell your property. The value-added tax, referred to as the *Impuesto al Valor Agregado* (IVA) tax, is assessed only on the construction of a property if it is a commercial property. The tax is approximately 15 percent of the value of the commercial building, while the acquisition tax hovers around 2 percent.

Pros and Cons of Owning a Mexican Corporation

Pros	Cons
1. You do not need a trust with the bank (a fideicomiso). 2. You do not need to pay an annual bank fee (about $500 a year) for you trust. 3. You can purchase multiple properties under one corporation. 4. You are entitled to a temporary resident visa, which can be renewed up to five years. 5. Your corporation can be 100-percent foreign-owned. 6. Labor is very cheap in Mexico.	1. It can be a lengthy process. 2. It can cost around $3,000 to obtain all the necessary documents 3. You must use your property for commercial purposes only. 4. You will be subject to a monthly tax filing and will be required to report income and outgo for which IVA taxes, capital gains taxes, and other taxes may be due. 5. You will pay the commercial rate for water, electricity, and other utilities, which is higher than residential rates.

Be wary of any real estate agent who encourages you to form a corporation if you are looking for a residential property and have no intention of using it for a business. You can get into seriously mucky waters if you try to get around setting up a trust with the bank, and it only puts you at risk for losing the title to your property — not to mention committing serious tax fraud. Unless it is clear you are opening a business, it is never recommended to purchase property in the restricted zone without using a trust. The cost of maintaining a trust each year is around $500, relatively cheap considering the financial obligations you may meet if you try to get around this rule. If anyone tries to tell you differently, find someone new to advise you.

Private Property

Private property includes single-family homes, timeshares, and condominiums. For the most part, the land you will be interested in buying will most likely be private. (To clarify, private property can still be located within the restricted zone, as can *ejidal* property). However, some condominium developments and other communities are also located on *ejidal* land, but if you are buying in one of these communities, the land has already been privatized. It is always wise to double-check, however, that the land has actually been privatized and that the proper notifications were made. It is important that the land is not being disputed like it was when the developer of the Baja Beach and Tennis Club in Ensenada began building. You can do this by checking with the Public Registry of Property and consulting with a specialist.

Condominiums

Condominiums are perhaps the most popular type of property in Mexico that foreigners purchase. Condo developments are abundant throughout oceanfront communities like Cancun, Los Cabos, and Puerto Vallarta. Many buyers are attracted to condo developments because they are fairly easy to use as a second or retirement home, and many of them resemble five-star resorts. These are becoming increasingly present in Mexico, as owning a condo unit requires little maintenance. Condos are ideal for retirees who are looking for limited upkeep obligations and luxury amenities. Investors also like the privacy and community-like atmosphere that often accompanies condo developments.

Condo developments and all the operations inside the development are generally run by the developer and are therefore completely private. That means the sewer and electrical system, along with all the roads, are maintained by the development through the use of a cooperative. This also goes for things like garbage disposal and landscaping. Technically, everyone owns the development, and residents pay a maintenance fee to upkeep and maintain all the common areas.

The most important thing to keep in mind when it comes to condo developments is the title. The developer must already have title to the property on which the development is built (or being built) in order for your investment to be a wise — not to mention legal — one. Investors should be very wary of purchasing condo units in a development where the developer does not have title to the property or the proper building permits.

If you invest in condominium development — especially if you are investing as a pre-sale where the development has not been built yet — without first ensuring that the developer holds the title to the land, you are setting yourself up for disaster. Investors in the Baja Beach and Tennis Club learned the hard way that forking over any money on a property where the land is not fully privatized — or in this case where the nature of the land was being disputed in court — is not a wise decision.

As with every real estate contract, your condo purchase contract should outline the details of your unit, including its dimensions and a description of the common areas (areas that are owned by everyone in the development), and list a description of the maintenance fees for your particular unit, among other things.

Most importantly with condo developments, ask for a copy of the title. If one cannot be produced for any reason, do not deposit a dime until it can. In most of the larger, well-known developments in popular areas, the issue of titles and permits is not one at all, and the developer has cleared everything far in advance of building.

CASE STUDY: A RETIREMENT HAVEN IN LAKE CHAPALA

When Suzanne Forrest and her husband moved to Lake Chapala in 1997, it was the affordable medical care that encouraged them to make the move. Her husband, suffering from Parkinson's disease, was in need of round-the-clock medical care — something that was not very affordable in the United States. Forrest, who had lived in Guatemala and is fluent in Spanish, considered her options south of the border.

Selling their home in an affluent neighborhood in Placitas, New Mexico, the Forrests relocated to Mexico and bought a home in Lake Chapala, located near Guadalajara. A popular retirement community, the area boasts excellent medical care, restaurants, water sports, entertainment, and many other amenities.

"I decided we should come down and check out what it would be like to live here," said Forrest. "I knew we could get affordable care, and knowing Mexican people, Guatemalan people, I knew it would be very personal and caring."

She and her husband considered renting at first but ultimately decided to buy a house and take advantage of the affordable real estate.

"We bought a house because we knew we would have handicapped facilities installed," she explained. "We didn't want to rent a place and then be asked to move after two or three years after having to put money into fixing it up."

Forrest found an affordable home for much less money than they sold the New Mexican house for, which enabled her to pocket the profit. Since she has bought her house, the value has nearly doubled, which will provide a considerable profit if she ever decides to sell. As an added bonus, she will not have to pay capital gains taxes on their sale because she has lived in their home for more than 2 years and it has been her primary residence.

In addition to affordable medical car, the Forrests also enjoy a low cost of living. She was also grateful she did not need to worry about paying for pricey air conditioning and heating like she had to in the U.S. The safety of the community was

CASE STUDY: A RETIREMENT HAVEN IN LAKE CHAPALA

also a big draw, as was the relaxed and friendly atmosphere. "It is probably a lot safer here than it is in the United States," she said. "I wouldn't worry at all about walking alone after dark in my neighborhood."

Another great aspect of life in Mexico is the cash economy. "Forget your plastic," Forrest said. "The only time you use it is if you go to buy a big-ticket item from a big store. Otherwise, if you go to the doctor, you pay cash and get a receipt." She also enjoys the proximity of grocery stores, medical care, and great restaurants offering a variety of cuisine.

Forrest notes that many foreigners may be turned off from the idea of buying property in Mexico because they believe they cannot own property outright, which is not the case. There is a very diverse population of foreigners and locals in Lake Chapala.

"We have diplomatic service people, foreign service people, a number of people who have worked with oil companies in Saudi Arabia — people who enjoy the opportunity to live in a place with a different culture," Forrest said.

After her husband's passing, she found comfort in the network of friends she has created while living in Lake Chapala. A former president of the Lake Chapala Society, Forrest keeps herself busy with organizing events for the *Viva la Musica!*, an association that organizes musical events and concert series. "The large expatriate community makes it a congenial place to live," she said. It has made a big impact on the area of Lake Chapala, volunteering for local organizations and raising money for causes like *Niños Incapacitados*, a group dedicated to helping disabled children.

Today, she very much enjoys her life south of the border. "People ask: 'What do you do down there?'" Forrest said. "Really, there are so many opportunities to get involved that is it hard not to get overcommitted."

She plans to stay put in Lake Chapala for as long as she can, she said.

"It's my home."

Timeshares

Timeshares are also very popular in Mexico, mostly for people who strictly want a vacation home without the obligations that come along with home ownership. Timeshare properties are widespread in the more tourist-driven areas of Mexico like Cabo San Lucas and Puerto Vallarta. Timeshares have been popular for decades, as investors are drawn to the ease and accessibility of owning one.

Unlike purchasing single-family homes and condominiums, buyers who purchase timeshare properties do not own the rights to the property. They are only entitled to the right of using the property at a specified time. As a result of the peaked interest in timeshares in the early 1990s, the government created national standards, known as *Normas Oficiales Mexicana* (NOM), to regulate timesharing and provide protection to timeshare buyers and investors. For example, developers are required to have an insurance policy on the timeshare property before presenting a contract to a buyer.

Through NOM, the government regulates timeshare sales of both completed developments and those in pre-sale. Pre-sales are quite common and involve the buyer putting down a deposit before the development is fully built. If you are considering buying a pre-sale timeshare, you should do the following:

- Check that the developer has title to the property and has acquired all the necessary building permits.

- Confirm that the developer has insurance on the development.

- Investigate the financial status and health of the developer. Research other properties the developer has built, and even approach owners of existing timeshares.

- Ensure that your contract contains a clause outlining the stipulations of the purchase, and a clause that explains the terms if the purchase falls through.

Your purchase contract with the developer should be very specific in regard to the details of the terms of use. It should include an explanation of the maintenance fees, your obligations when swapping out your timeshare with another owner, and the exact property that is considered shared. The contract should also stipulate what happens if your timeshare is not available for some reason during your determined block of time. Many investors may not realize that it is the obligation of the timeshare to find a similar and acceptable timeshare property if your property is not accessible to you.

Being naïve to the process can put you at risk for losing your deposit if the developer is not financially secure, or if he or she has not obtained the proper documents and permits to build a timeshare property.

Because timeshares are shared property, and you do not own the rights to that property, they appeal mostly to people looking for a place to spend a few weeks out of the year. The great thing about timeshares is the low commitment to upkeep, and the access to luxurious amenities like pools and golf courses. The downside is you will be limited to a specific time frame to use the property, and you often have to choose your weeks well in advance.

Single-Family Homes

Next to timeshares and condo developments, single-family homes are popular choices among foreign investors. Although less common, many investors find the privacy and sole-ownership factors as a draw to single-family homes over shared residences. On the other hand, single-family homes are not as appealing to many foreigners compared to condo developments and time-share for the obvious reason: Houses are expensive to maintain, and they require a lot of work. Like the large popular developments in the more touristy areas of Mexico, residential single houses for sale by owners are listed with a real estate agent, often on a multiple-listing service Web site.

Unlike timeshare and condo developments, there is no developer or builder who has obtained permits and the title to the property for single-family homes. It is your responsibility as a buyer to investigate the status of the home you are considering and establish the following:

- Is the property located within the restricted zone?

- Does the seller have the title to the property and, therefore, the right to sell the property?

- Is the home already in a trust with the bank?

Determining if the seller holds the title to the property should be your no. 1 one priority before you proceed with anything else. You can do this by performing a title search (with the help of a closing agent or attorney) on the property, which will determine who officially holds the title to the property. If it is not the seller, then he or she does not have the right to sell the property to you.

For those investors looking for more privacy, a single-family home may be ideal. There are lots of beautiful beachfront villas and cottages that dot Mexico's coastline, in addition to homes in smaller towns and villages in the interior of the country.

Unimproved Land

In addition to single-family homes, timeshares, and condominium developments, private property also includes unimproved or raw land, which will be luring to buyers interested in building a home or a commercial business. In Mexico, most communities are developments, and raw land within these developments is often already incorporated into the drainage, water, and electrical system. Should you venture to the outskirts of these developments, it is still possible to acquire raw land to build on, but be aware that you may need to build your own drainage, water, and electrical system to sustain your home. If the unimproved land is within the restricted zone, you may also be required by the Ministry of Foreign Affairs to acquire the land and build on it within two years of purchase. This requirement is to prevent people from simply buying and selling land, and instead encourages new construction and growth.

It can be somewhat challenging to gain permission to build on land that has no development and is not part of a subdivision that is owned by a developer. It is wise to look for empty lots of land that are within an existing development with road access, water, and electricity, and you will not be left with the challenging task of creating a self-sustaining system. The government tends to frown upon foreigners purchasing random plots of land that are not already at least partially developed or part of a subdivision, and thus the process can be challenging.

Comparing Your Options

	Pros	Cons
Timeshares	Minimal obligations to maintenance; easy to manage; great to swap with other time-share owners; waste disposal, landscaping, etc. taken care of; less expensive than a condo or private home.	Access is limited to a particular time of year; sharing your property with other users; limited privacy; shared common space; fees
Condominiums	Minimal obligations to maintenance; easy to manage; waste disposal, landscaping, etc. taken care of; unlike a timeshare, you own property rights and title.	Limited privacy; shared common space; maintenance fees; more expensive than a timeshare or private home.
Single-Family Homes	Much more private than condo or time-share developments; no maintenance fees unless in a planned community; ability to use at your own discretion.	Maintenance and upkeep at your own expense; no access to common property like a pool, gym, stores, etc., unless the property is in a planned community development.
Unimproved Land	Ability to build a custom home; no maintenance fees; privacy.	Involved process to obtain permits; establishing self-sustaining systems; cost and time of construction; you may be required to develop on the land within two years.

Public Property

Public property is property that is owned by Mexico as a country, and includes things like water, beaches, and particular parts of the land. Because public property belongs to the nation as a whole, any property categorized as public cannot be sold to anyone. The most significant part of this restriction to foreign investors is the fact that the first 20 meters of property located on a coastline or beach is located in the federal zone, which is part of public property. So, if you are planning on buying beachfront property, you will have to get confirmation that your lot is not inclusive of any property technically located in the federal zone. Most beachfront properties are built farther enough from the end of the 20 meters, but it is always wise to double check the zone specifics of your property.

Residential vs. Commercial

All property — condominium, single family, raw land, and time-shares — is further classified as residential or non-residential. According to Mexican law, commercial property includes:

- Timeshares

- Any property to be used for commercial use, like a bed and breakfast, a restaurant, or a retail store

- Development properties that have not yet been divided and sold to individual investors

There are additional properties that fall into the non-residential category, including foreclosed homes, but your property will most likely fall into one of these three categories. All other properties, including condominiums and single-family houses, are considered residential properties.

Regardless of the type of property you purchase, you must register your property with the Property Tax Office and the Public Registry of Property. If the nature of the property is not clear — if you do not know if it is technically in the restricted zone, for instance — you can inquire with the Ministry of Foreign Affairs, and they are required to respond within two weeks of your inquiry.

CASE STUDY: THE ROAD TO CASA LUNA

In 1994, Dianne Kushner was itching to start over. Like many people who wind up in Mexico, Kushner always loved the country's beautiful beaches, relaxed atmosphere, and affordable living. She also lost a number of friends that year and, as she said, "I decided life was too short, and I wanted another adventure."

That adventure turned out to be opening a bed and breakfast in the charming, sleepy town of San Miguel de Allende. Deciding a move to Mexico would suit her well, Kushner sold her home in northern California and headed to San Miguel, a town she favored since visiting the area in the 1970s.

In 1994, San Miguel was not quite as built up as it is today, and Kushner saw a great opportunity. "At the time, there were not many different places to stay," she said.

A realtor helped Kushner find a property for her B&B in the historic district of San Miguel, which is now a large tourist attraction, thanks to its cobblestone streets, historic churches, and charming shops.

The property she purchased had been on the market for some time, and the price was just right. Kushner used part of her profit from the sale of her home in California toward a down payment and renovations on the new B&B property, which was five times the size.

"I opened in 1996 with four rooms and $150 left in my pocket," she said. "The property had good bones, but it was kind of ugly. It had white walls and orange shag carpeting — it had been Americanized."

CASE STUDY: THE ROAD TO CASA LUNA

After $100,000 in renovations, Kushner restored some of that old-world Mexican charm. "I knew I wanted the look to reflect the romance of Old Mexico: lots of antiques, rustic furniture," she said. With that vision, Kushner created a luxurious B&B that *Travel + Leisure* magazine touts as, "One of the world's most fabulous and unknown hotels."

As with almost every investment, there existed some risk in Kushner's move from the safety of her northern California existence to the relative unknown in another country. Her risk was her lack of a long-term business plan to attract customers and advertise her business. She also did not know much of the language. This did not deter her from continuing with business as usual, however. "I just kind of jumped right in," she said.

As for getting business, "First off, I was very prompt in returning phone calls," she said. "People felt comfortable speaking to an American. I could respond to them and tell them where to eat and shop. I also met other people who have bed and breakfasts in other towns."

Slowly, Kushner built her business from referrals from other B&Bs and by word-of-mouth. Eventually, magazines and newspapers became interested in her B&B as the popularity of San Miguel began to grow, and it became a hot spot for Americans and other foreigners to vacation.

"The town has changed an awful lot," Kushner said. "San Miguel de Allende seems to have hit the publicity circuit about five or six years ago."

Eventually, Kushner bought several adjoining properties, which include cozy guest rooms equipped with fireplaces and featherbeds, a large indoor/outdoor dining area surrounded by lush gardens, and a lounge from which to watch the gorgeous sunset. She also recently acquired a ranch outside the town, which she uses for cooking classes to attract Americans looking for the increasingly popular learning vacation.

Although Kushner took a leap of faith with her move to Mexico and her business, she recommends that people considering moving to Mexico, whether it be to relax and enjoy or to start a business, take a more calculated approach. "I suggest you come and stay here, renting a place for about six months," she advised. "That way, you will understand the different neighborhoods."

Since her move, the town has nearly doubled in population and has dozens of new businesses. The growth speaks volumes to the trend and the exponential growth that the country has seen in the past 20 years. The town now boasts many Americanized amenities, including Starbucks, Walmart, and even a Costco Wholesale.

CASE STUDY: THE ROAD TO CASA LUNA

With guests from around the world, Kushner has seen her business grow tremendously over the past 13 years she has been in business, and she finally feels as if she is in the right place. "I am kind of just enjoying my life very much here now," she said.

For more information on Casa Luna, visit **www.casaluna.com**.

CHAPTER 2

Understanding the Investment Process

The real estate market in Mexico has boomed in recent years as baby boomers are increasingly turning to Mexico to retire, and all types of investors are taking advantage of the affordable living south of the border to make a smart investment. While the real estate market in the United States and elsewhere around the world tends to be unpredictable at times, the real estate market in Mexico continues to thrive and has seen a solid, steady increase for the past decade.

> "Mexico is a wonderful and very beautiful country. A property purchase in Mexico can be just as safe and secure as in the United States or Canada, if it is done correctly," said Linda Neil, founder of The Settlement Company.

The buying trend south of the border can be attributed to a number of factors. Beginning in the early 1990s, the Mexican government began reforming laws and regulations that opened the doors to foreign investment, which in turn allowed investors to feel more comfortable purchasing property in the country. Prior to the establishment of regulations and protection by the Mexican government, investors essentially took a chance when purchasing property and had to do the best they could to ensure their purchase was legal. It was a confusing process full of loopholes that increased the potential for investors losing out on thousands of dollars. Because of several high-profile horror stories that made their way to U.S. media, American investors were especially wary of even considering investing in real estate in Mexico — and rightfully so.

Today, the process gets smoother by the day. Although the foreign investment industry is fairly young, as the demand for property has grown, the government has worked to streamline the process to make it as easy as possible for their neighbors to the north (and elsewhere around the world).

The Process of Purchasing in Mexico

Contrary to some claims, the process of purchasing real estate in Mexico is not unlike the process of purchasing in the United States and other similar countries, with a few significant differences that are crucial to understand. Below is a list of the general steps to purchasing property in Mexico, all of which will be discussed in greater detail in later chapters.

General Steps in the Real Estate Investment Process

- **Select a property you are interested in.** The property is most likely represented by a real estate agent, who will facilitate the initial discussion and answer questions. If you really want to be on top of things — which you should be if you are really interested in the property — start researching the area.

- **Determine the nature of the property and if you will need a bank trust.** Is the land you are interested in *ejidal*, government owned, or private property? If it is private property, is it located in the restricted zone? Determining these answers will determine the various requirements for purchasing.

- **Make an offer.** As in the United States, some buyers and sellers agree on a verbal offer; however, the only way to ensure that the offer is officially accepted is with a written contract. In Mexico, the contract is called the Offer to Purchase and will outline all the provisions of the deal. At this stage, you should not part in any down payment money until you have taken ample time to review the contract with your closing agent or attorney.

- **Make a deposit to a third-party escrow service.** Escrow is an account, usually held with a bank or a neutral third party, in which a buyer deposits funds that will be held for a period of time while certain conditions are met, and the terms of a contract are decided upon and executed. Escrow services are limited in Mexico. Some banks and credit companies that are recognized as established in the industry offer escrow services but in general, escrow companies do not exist in Mexico. Buyers should never deposit funds to any company that claims to be an escrow service unless it has a legitimate U.S. trust account. If you hire a closing agent, the company can often hold the deposit in escrow for you; certain reputable real estate agencies offer escrow services as well.

- **Get a trust, or *fideicomiso*, if your property is in the restricted zone.** Foreigners are unable to directly purchase property in the restricted zone, and if you are purchasing property within this geographical area, a bank will serve as a trustee between you and the property, and essentially lease you the land. This also includes applying for a permit with the Ministry of Foreign Affairs.

- **Sign a promissory agreement.** This essentially binds you to purchasing the property and serves as your contract. If your property is in the restricted zone, you will sign the promissory agreement with the seller and obtain permits through the bank that holds your trust; if your property is outside the restricted zone, you will sign the contract directly with the seller.

- **Conduct a title search and obtain the land deed.** This is a key step in the process. A closing agent or title insurance company will facilitate the title search and determine if the seller holds the title to the property. A *notario publico* will also conduct a basic title search, but it is best to hire a closing agent or title company to conduct a more thorough search. Buyers are highly advised to obtain title insurance, which protects against monetary losses if a deal falls through because there is an issue with the title.

- **Submit a series of tax and property documents.** This includes the Certificate of No Encumbrances, which is issued through the Public Registry of Property where the property is located and is based upon a review of the seller's title document. This also includes the Certificate of No Tax Liability, which details the property tax payments on the property. Although the seller is responsible for these, the buyer should at least be aware that these documents are needed to complete the sale.

- **Conduct a property appraisal.** An official appraiser will determine the value of your property and your land, which will eventually play a role in determining your property taxes.

- **Sign the final contract, the Purchase-Sales Agreement.** After you sign the final contract, the title and deed will officially be transferred to you.

- **Close the deal.** Here is where you will pay any remaining fees, including those to the *notario publico*, your closing agent if you have one, and your real estate agent, as well as the acquisition tax.

As you can see, the process is quite straightforward, but it also involves a number of additional steps that are particular to purchasing real estate in Mexico that many foreigners may not be familiar with. It is often easiest to understand these additional steps by comparing them to the process you are familiar with:

The Major Differences in the Real Estate Investment Process between Mexico and the United States

- Foreigners are unable to directly purchase property in the restricted zone. Because most beachfront property is in the restricted zone, the Mexican government reformed Article 27 of the Mexican Constitution to allow foreigners to be able to purchase property in the restricted zone through the use of a bank trust, a *fideicomiso*.

- Real estate agents are not required to be licensed in Mexico, so anyone can technically be a real estate agent, but well-established ones are registered with The Association of

Mexican Real Estate Professionals (*La Asociación Mexicana de Profesionales Inmobiliarios*, or AMPI). Because not all real estate agents are required to be licensed, the safest way to ensure an agent is reliable and trustworthy is to check they are listed with the AMPI, which recognizes only professional and established people in the industry. Neil explained: "Through its agreements with the National Association of Realtors® (NAR) a Mexican agent who is a member of AMPI is entitled to use the symbol and the Realtor® designation."

- Real estate transactions generally involve two to three contracts: the promissory agreement, the purchase-sales agreement, and the final contract or deed, which may be a fee simple deed — the purchase does not require a bank trust, and the buyer may purchase directly from the seller.

- Closing costs are significantly higher in Mexico than in the United States because there are significantly more fees and documents to obtain during the process. Typically, closing costs, including fees for various required documents, are typically between 4 to 8 percent of the value of the property but can be higher. The higher costs are offset by lower property and other taxes paid throughout the year.

- Most investors purchase homes with cash in Mexico, although cross-the-border mortgage companies and banks have significantly increased opportunities for investors to finance real estate purchases in foreign countries.

- Escrow companies are hard to come by in Mexico. U.S. title and escrow companies offer escrow services to foreign buyers, and using one of these companies is becoming more common. "Trying to get a Mexican bank to set up an escrow account is a real challenge (for a foreign buyer)," explained Neil, who advises all her clients to use a U.S.-based, FDIC-insured account.

• The notary public officials are appointed by the government and are most often experienced attorneys who prepare the deed, do a basic title search, and review the title and certificates. They also oversee the process of transferring the title to the buyer and will identify any problems with the title and inform the buyer.

• Foreigners are unable to purchase government-owned land, or *ejidal* land, unless it is privatized first. *Ejidal* land is government-owned land that is leased to large groups of *ejidatarios*, or Mexican nationals, who farm the land and fish the surrounding waters. Because so much valuable property is technically *ejidal* land, the government made it possible for *ejidos* to privatize the land and then sell it to an investor, or someone outside the *ejido*. The process of purchasing *ejidal* land is long and involved.

According to the U.S. State Department, the number of Americans permanently living in Mexico is double that of the number of Americans living there ten years ago.

As with any transaction, it is always advisable to seek professional guidance from the very beginning to avoid any time-consuming hold-ups or worse, illegitimate transactions. Prior to the current laws, many foreigners were wrongly led to believe they could purchase land when they could not, that the seller obtained the official title, and that the process was legal. Now, with the process more streamlined and clear, instances of people losing out on money and time have decreased dramatically; however, it is still wise to be aware of all the necessary requirements so your transaction is smooth and headache-free. One way to do this is to be familiar with the Mexican legal system and the role it will play in your investment.

The Ins and Outs of Mexican Law

Today, with the help of a few revised and new laws, foreigners can enjoy much more protection when purchasing property south of the border. While your closing agent and real estate agent — as well as other professionals you will work with during the investment process — can explain the legalities of your purchase to you, it is wise to be at least somewhat familiar with the framework of the Mexican legal system before purchasing property. A brief understanding of the legal system will enable you to feel more comfortable throughout the whole process to make it go as smoothly as possible.

The Mexican Constitution

Like the U.S. law, a federal constitution — as well as civil and state laws for each state in the country — forms Mexican law. The Mexican Constitution, established in 1917 during the Mexican Revolution, outlines a handful of key laws that regulate the rights of foreign investors and define the nature and types of land throughout the country. There have been several revisions and additions to the constitution that apply to real estate law, further adding to the foundation of the laws that govern the process of purchasing property in Mexico. Article 27 and Article 33 speak particularly to foreigners and their rights when it comes to purchasing property and living in Mexico.

The Mexican Constitution determines the difference between foreigners and Mexican citizens. The Constitution defines Mexicans as:

A. "All persons born of Mexican parents

B. Naturalized foreigners

C. Foreigners who have children born in Mexico, unless they preserve their nationality by proper declaration."

If you do not meet one of these three conditions, you will be considered a foreigner in the eyes of the government and therefore subject to the restrictions of foreigners. These restrictions include directly purchasing property in the restricted zone.

Article 27 states that the government owns all land, minerals, and water in the country and possesses the authority to establish property as private and to grant concessions for water and minerals. Although the article determines the rights of citizens to own and sell private property, the article also determines that foreigners cannot directly purchase the following property because it is owned by the nation:

• Restricted zone property

• All natural resources, including the water

While the government prohibits the direct purchase of any property within the restricted zone by a foreign investor, the property may be purchased in the following ways:

• Through the use of a *fideicomiso* or a trust

• Through a Mexican corporation. Your transaction is then considered "fee simple," which allows direct ownership of property in the restricted zone for Mexican corporations using the property for commercial purposes

Additionally, Article 27 defines *ejidal* property.

Article 33 determines that foreigners do not have the right to participate in Mexican politics, which includes elections, political rallies, and demonstrations.

The Calvo Clause

While the difference between a foreigner and a national may seem obvious, it is important to point out that although foreigners are not Mexican citizens, they are still required to comply with the Mexican legal system while they are in the country.

The Calvo Clause states that as a foreigner, you are subject to the laws and regulations of Mexico when you are in the country, regardless of your residency status. The clause is intended to prevent foreigners from seeking legal protection from their home country (or any other country) in the event of a legal dispute. In the eyes of a Mexican court, you will be considered a citizen of Mexico in any arbitration or legal dispute.

The Foreign Investment Law

The Foreign Investment Law, originally known as the Act to Promote Mexican Foreign Investment and Regulate Foreign Investment, speaks specifically about foreign investment and complements the Mexican Constitution that initially recognized the government's involvement of foreign interest in the country's property and land.

The sequential revisions to this act throughout the late 1980s and 1990s opened the doors even further to foreign investment and established opportunities for foreigners to purchase real estate in Mexico for either residential or commercial use. The Foreign Investment Law, revised in 1993, elaborated further on the specifics of real estate investment by foreigners and eased the restrictions on foreign investors that once existed. With that came much shorter waiting periods for required documents and fewer loopholes in the process. The revisions were a push from the government to make investing in real estate more appealing to foreigners.

In general, the Foreign Investment Law states:

- Foreigners are able to purchase land in the restricted zone for non-residential, commercial purposes through a Mexican corporation, which can be foreign owned. In other words, you can buy property for commercial use (such as for a bed and breakfast, restaurant, or retail store) if you are part of a business. None of the parties in your corporation need to be Mexican nationals to be recognized as a corporation.

- *Fideicomisos* acquired through a bank can be renewed every 50 years, instead of every 30, as previous forms of the law stated.

- Foreign buyers must agree to the Calvo Clause before they can acquire a *fideicomiso* with the bank. For buyers purchasing property outside the restricted zone, they must agree in writing with the Calvo Clause in order to legally purchase property.

- Foreigners may purchase property for residential use outside the restricted zone through a process called fee simple. In these transactions, buyers do not need to seek a trust from the bank, but must register their property with the Ministry of Foreign Relations.

More specifically, the Foreign Investment Law defines a foreigner as:

- "An individual or entity of any nationality other than Mexican; and foreign entities with no legal standing."

Furthermore, it is defined as:

- "Participation by foreign investors, in any percentage, in the capital stock of Mexican companies

- Investments by Mexican companies in which foreign capital has majority interest

- Participation by foreign investors in activities and acts contemplated herein."

The Ministry of Foreign Affairs

The Ministry of Foreign Affairs handles citizenship, naturalization, and establishment of foreigners in the country. It is very important to follow the said requirements by the ministry, which involves applying for various permits to establish yourself as a potential property owner or a Mexican corporation.

The Ministry of Foreign Affairs is responsible for granting the required permits to buy property and/or land in any part of the country. Specifically, Article 10A of the Foreign Investment Law requires foreigners who are purchasing property within the restricted zone to apply for a permit from the Ministry of Foreign Affairs to be officially recognized by the country and to obtain a trust from a bank. If the property you are purchasing is already in a trust with a bank, which would be the case in many resales by and to foreigners, sellers are required to instruct the trustee bank to assign the rights in the trust to a new buyer, which transfers the title and the trust to the new buyer.

Prior to the revisions of the investment law, this process was anything but quick and even less clear. According to Article 14 of law,

> "Any application to obtain a permit must be resolved up upon by the Ministry of Foreign Affairs within five business days following the date of the application with the competent central administrative unit or within thirty days if submitted before the state office of said Ministry; otherwise, approval shall be deemed to have been granted."

The article is significant because it creates a time frame in which the Ministry needs to respond to the permit application, which is a great thing for you as an investor as it eliminates the endless waiting periods that (sometimes) previously existed.

The Ministry of Foreign Affairs will play an important role in your Mexican investment, as it determines your compliance with the foreign investment law. If you are not in compliance, the ministry can deny your permit, and you will not be able to obtain the title to your property or to obtain the trust with a Mexican bank if you are buying in the restricted zone. More often than not, though, foreign buyers do not run into any issues with the ministry and breeze through this phase of the process. The ministry continues to revise their policies to make the process of purchasing property easier for foreign investors and also to encourage international and foreign interest in Mexico.

Public Registry of Property

When you purchase land or property in Mexico, it should be registered with the Public Registry of Property to be officially recognized by the government to give notice to third parties of the ownership of the property. Your closing agent should take care of this for you after you sign the deed to the property.

National Foreign Investment Registry

According to Title Seven, Article 32 of the Foreign Investment Law, Mexican companies that are owned (or partially owned) by foreign investors must register their corporation with the National Foreign Investment Registry. Corporations and companies are required to register the nature and structure of their company and financial activity, among other details.

The purpose of the registry is to chronicle all foreign investment activity. If you are forming a corporation or legally becoming part of one, your attorney will advise you on the details of registering your company.

The Federal Civil Code

The Civil Code establishes the nature of a contract. Logically, the Civil Code defines a contract as an agreement between two or more parties. More significantly, the Civil Code states that all contracts regarding the transfer of real property must be signed in the presence of a *notario publico* before they can be officially recognized. Furthermore, the Civil Code provides the guidelines for the new owner to register his or her property with the Public Registry of Property to give notice to third parties of the ownership of the land.

Agrarian Law

Agrarian Law governs *ejidal* land and establishes the right for an *ejidatario* to sell his or her parcel of the *ejido* for a profit.

As Mexico began to cultivate its tourism industry and realize the potential of its real estate, the government made reforms that opened many doors for foreign investors. In the 1970s, corporations were allowed to lease the *ejidal* land to benefit themselves and their companies by farming the land. *Ejidatarios*, naturally, revolted against this, as they saw no benefit to being forced off their land with no compensation.

In the early 1990s, the Mexican government amended the Constitution to acknowledge the ownership and property rights of individual *ejidos* and their portion of the land. This enabled *ejidatarios* to sell their parcels of land for a profit for the first time through the process of privatization, discussed in detail in Chapter 1. *Ejidatarios* are legally allowed to sell their individual parcels of land — provided the rest of the *ejidatarios* approve — or the entire *ejido* may sell the land with a collective consensus.

Many *ejidatarios* have taken full advantage of this, as they can benefit significantly from the sale of such valuable land. Agrarian law also allows *ejidatarios* to take out a loan against their land and lease their land to farmers outside their *ejido* to use the land.

Tax Laws

Navigating taxes when you own a home or property outside your native country can be confusing. Especially if your Mexican home will not be your primary residence, it is always best to consult with an attorney or financial advisor in your country first to determine the tax implications of your purchase.

As for Mexican tax laws, the most significant would probably be the Mexico Tax Revenue Code and the U.S. Tax Relief Act, which both speak specifically to foreigners who own property or do business in Mexico. According to the Tax Revenue Code, Mexican nationals and foreigners living in and owning property in Mexico can receive a significant tax break on the profit made from the sale of the property if it was a primary residence and if the foreigner or Mexican national is a tax resident of Mexico. For Mexican nationals, the tax break is offered regardless of the amount of the profit. For U.S. citizens, a tax break is available only if Mexico is the primary residence of the seller.

The U.S. Tax Relief Act, passed in the late 1990s, provides significant tax relief for homeowners, as it enables one to deduct the interest one pays for mortgage on his or her U.S. taxes. Fortunately for foreign investors, this also applies to homes in Mexico — even if they serve as second homes.

In the context of a buyer/seller situation, the following taxes will apply to your transaction:

Acquisitions tax: Also called the transfer tax, the acquisitions tax is paid by the buyer and is currently around 2 percent of the total value of the property.

Capital gains tax: Paid by the seller, this can be more than 30 percent of the profit value made from the sale.

In general, property taxes are significantly lower than they are in the United States. Taxes on rental income, however, can be significantly higher. Taxes will be discussed in greater detail in Chapter 3.

CHAPTER 3

How to Decide if Buying is Right For You

Owning a home is a big responsibility. Owning two homes is a *huge* responsibility. Mexico has become a popular retirement location for baby boomers and investors who are simply looking for a second abode to serve as an affordable vacation home. Whether it is for the relaxing lifestyle, the beauty of the beaches, or the affordability of many properties throughout Mexico, the trend of purchasing south of the border is only getting stronger.

With the financial and real estate boom of the mid-2000s came a surge of Americans buying property in Mexico. Prices for beachfront property were relatively low compared to similar property on the California coast. With the crash of the real estate market in 2008, Mexico has seen a slight dip in property purchases, as many Americans were forced to tighten their belts when it came to spending money and buying real estate.

Since then, property prices for vacation or second homes have not increased dramatically. It is still very affordable to invest in a piece of property in Mexico — provided you purchase property that is not more than your price range, and you consider all the expenses that come along with owning a second home.

While many smart investors look at their Mexico purchase as just that — an investment — there are also those buyers who do not take the time to consider their purchase and weigh their options. Some people go to Mexico on vacation or to visit a friend and fall in love with a beachfront bungalow, or get swept away by the appeal of a brand new beachfront condo with five-star amenities. They want to purchase property without fully thinking about it thoroughly. The appeal of the aesthetics of Mexico can often mask the complexity of the purchasing process and the details you should consider before investing in property, and can ultimately lead you into purchasing something you may not be able to afford.

Without sitting down and thinking about all the things that come along with home ownership, especially all the financial obligations, you are potentially getting in over your head. There are a considerable number of options to weigh and factors to contemplate before deciding to purchase real estate in Mexico — or any country for that matter. In this chapter, you will find discussions of questions you should ask yourself before you purchase property, including:

- How will I finance my purchase?

- What kind of property am I interested in?

- What is my budget, and what can I afford?

- How often will I use the property?

- Do I need to rent out the property when I am not there to offset costs?

- Do I need to sell my current home to finance my Mexico purchase?

- What kind of taxes are associated with a Mexican property?

- What will it cost me to live in Mexico and run my home?

This chapter is designed to help you answer these questions.

How Will I Finance My Purchase?

This is perhaps the first thing potential investors should ask themselves. A significant part of the crash of the U.S. real estate market in 2008 can be attributed to buyers purchasing property they could not afford. Mortgage companies and banks willingly lent money to less than ideal borrowers who did not have the financial means to pay it back, and many people bought homes simply because they could. If you are considering purchasing a home in any country, you should not consider doing so simply because a mortgage company is offering you a deal you cannot resist. That logic, or illogic, is what got everyone into such a mess in the end.

While almost 95 percent of property purchased in Mexico is purchased with cash, mortgaging property is becoming increasingly popular as more mortgage companies in the United States, especially, are beginning to offer financing to U.S. citizens looking to buy property south of the border. We are also beginning to see mortgage companies and other credit institutions that specialize only in mortgages for Mexican purchases. ConfiCasa Mortgage International, for instance, specializes in cross-the-border financing and offers a variety of different loan programs to qualified applicants.

Chapter 10 will discuss various financing options in detail.

What Kind of Property Am I Interested In?

Prices can vary greatly, depending on the type of property you are interested in. First, it is best to establish what you are looking for in your Mexican purchase. To recap, there are four general types of properties: condos, timeshares, single-family houses, and raw or undeveloped land. In addition to timeshares, condos are the most popular property type among foreign investors, and often the most expensive. Single-family homes are popular for those interested in a more private setting, and undeveloped or raw land is appealing for those looking to build a house or a commercial business.

What Is My Budget and What Can I Afford?

This question is particularly important to answer before you even begin to look at property. Determining a budget will determine what areas to search for property, how much you will be required to put own for a down payment, and what your closing costs and maintenance expenses will be. It is helpful to come up with a price range, which will allow you have some leeway when looking at different properties.

The typical amount required as a down payment is a minimum of 20 percent in Mexico, which can be a significant amount of money, especially if you are purchasing property without selling your existing home. If you plan to use your property as a vacation home (or a second residence), the interest on your mortgage may be tax deductible. You will, however, be subject to capital gains taxes if you sell your home.

Here is a basic formula to give you an idea of your average monthly payment on a $150,000 property with a 30-year mortgage at 8 percent interest.

Price of the property: $150,000
Length of mortgage: 30 years
Down payment: 20 percent, or $30,000
Amount mortgaged: $120,000
Interest rate: 8 percent
Average yearly property taxes: $750 (at a 0.5 percentage rate)
Average monthly property taxes: $62

Total average monthly payment: $942 (roughly $880 mortgage payment plus $62 in taxes)

Your payment will greatly depend on the terms of your mortgage. Property taxes are quite low in Mexico and average less than 1 percent of the value of your property per year.

CASE STUDY: MEXICO'S REAL ESTATE LURES FATHER/SON BUSINESS PARTNERS

Recently, David Biondolillo crossed the border from Rosari- to Beach to San Diego, California, to see Martin Scorsese's documentary of the Rolling Stones, which was only playing in limited theaters. "Other than that, for me, I would never cross the border!" Biondolillo said. "Whatever I want is down here. I am happy."

Biondolillo's adventure to Mexico began in 2005, when his adult son, Kanoa, prompted his dad to make a move. The two worked as business partners selling Los Angeles real estate. "My son said, 'We'd better move, or we are not going to be in business in three years,'" he said.

After considering Central America, the Biondolillos decided what they were looking for — an easier and more affordable lifestyle — was right across the border. A family member had recently bought two properties in Mexico: an empty lot in Ensenada on which she built a house, and a townhouse in Rosarito. It prompted Biondolillo and his son to consider doing the same.

They started with Ensenada and Rosarito and immediately noticed a trend. "We noticed that something was going on," Biondolillo said. "Things were really booming. Buildings were being built, condominiums were being graded." Soon after, the Biondolillos found their place in the local real estate scene, founding Baja123 Real Estate, a company specializing in completed and pre-construction property in the Baja Peninsula.

Biondolillo also found the laidback Mexican way of living appealing, and built his business from talking to locals and developers he met along the way. He eventually ran into the developer of The Residences at Playa Blanca, a 250-room hotel and condo development, which he now represents as a realtor.

Biondolillo took advantage of the relatively inexpensive beachfront property and bought and sold an ocean-view plot in Playas, which he profited nicely from. While he waits for renovations to be completed on his new condo, which he plans to move into, he rents a four-bedroom, four-bath home in the Baja area with a large yard and beach access for about $2,000 a month. Back home, the same property would easily be four or five times that amount.

Though Biondolillo says there is a cost that accompanies coastal living, property is much cheaper. A $5-million condo in La Jolla, California, for instance, costs about $500,000 in Rosarito. Biondolillo also finds the cost of living much cheaper, like medical care and housekeeping. He recently had $15,000 worth of dental work done for about $3,000, and his housekeeper only charges $40 a month.

**CASE STUDY: MEXICO'S REAL ESTATE LURES
FATHER/SON BUSINESS PARTNERS**

Biondolillo remains quite content with his life in Baja. He enjoys the luxury of living near the beach in a brand new condo, the warm weather, the inexpensive food and medical care, and the easy access to American stores like Walmart. He is encouraging of anyone thinking of purchasing property and moving to Mexico, especially to Baja. "Out of all of Mexico — the places Americans want to come to — my area is most economical right now," he said.

To find out more on Baja real estate, visit **www.baja123.com**.

How Often Will I Use My Property?

The answer to this question will help determine what kind of property you will want. If you are planning on using your property for more than a few weeks a year, you can rule out a time-share. If you plan on spending more than six months a year at your Mexican home, you will have to consider the visa requirements. Your immigration status will depend on how long you plan to stay in Mexico each year.

- If you are staying less than six months a year, you will need to apply for a short-term, non-immigrant visa.

- If you are staying longer than six months a year, you will be required to apply for a long-term, immigrant visa.

- If you plan to eventually establish residency in Mexico, which may be the case if you plan to live full-time in Mexico, you will apply for an immigrant permit, which grants you permanent residency. You will have to prove a minimum income to gain residency.

Chapter 11 will further discuss visa requirements.

CASE STUDY: A NEW LEASE ON LIFE

It has been 15 years of fun for Rose and Ronnie Simcic. Since 1993, the couple has enjoyed taking vacations to their trailer on an oceanfront lot in an RV park in the small fishing town of Los Barriles, located on the Baja Peninsula close to Los Cabos. For $300 a month, the Simcics rent a 15-foot trailer that they visit a few times a year.

Sitting quietly on the Sea of Cortez, Los Barriles is a quaint fishing village located about an hour from the Los Cabos area. The area was once little known among foreigners, who flocked to Cabo San Lucas for the high-rise, luxurious condo developments. These days, some investors are looking for a quieter, lower pro-file area with affordable housing prices and beautiful beaches.

Los Barriles is proving to be such a place, and the Simcics have seen an in-creasing number of foreigners buy property in the area. Many are vacationers who spend just part of the year in the sleepy fishing village, but many are retir-ees who live in the area full time. Interestingly, the Simcics noticed the area is a draw particularly for retired U.S. fire and policemen and their families, who enjoy the affordability of much of the real estate. Because Los Barriles is not as popular — at least yet — as areas like Cabo, the real estate is still very afford-able for retirees and people on a limited income.

The Simcics have known this for years and initially began spending time in Mex-ico to take escape the daily grind of life in Los Angeles. The couple purchased a trailer and makes the journey south of the border during the spring and fall to take in a little serenity and to go fishing. As boating and fishing enthusiasts, the Simcics are active fishers when they are in Los Barriles and often catch up to 50 pounds of fish to bring back to their home in Los Angeles. While in Los Barriles, the couple also enjoys their catch of the day, and will often take the fish they have caught to a local restaurant, where the restaurant is happy to prepare fish any way they would like for as little as $7.

Fishing is a big part of the Simcics' vacation time in Mexico. When they are not out to eat at a local restaurant, enjoying their day's catch, they often visit with friends and enjoy a cookout or a barbeque. "Usually nobody is uptight," Ronnie said, "because nobody is working!"

The best part about Los Barriles, said the Simcics, is the peaceful and serene atmosphere that seems to radiate throughout the small village. "The water's

CASE STUDY: A NEW LEASE ON LIFE

blue, the stars shine," Rose said. "We call 9 p.m. Baja midnight because everyone goes to bed by then."

The next best thing is the great food and authentic Mexican restaurants. "It is better to go to places that are Mexican-owned, where you can get a decent price for breakfast," Rose said. "And the best place to get dinner is from the street vendors. They open up their backyards and make a restaurant! American places have California prices, so Mexican is the way to go." The supermarkets are also great and have fresh, local food at affordable prices, she added.

And when she wants to mingle with friends and locals and get a little exercise, Rose heads over to a $2 exercise class, held under a nearby hut, or *palapa*. The Simcics also take road trips to Cabo San Lucas, where they visit friends and access affordable medical care.

The laidback lifestyle is what drew the Simcics to Los Barriles more than a decade ago, and they plan to continue to enjoy their affordable vacation home for as long as they can. They hope to someday retire to the area and buy some property. For now, they enjoy the luxury of packing up and going back home at the end of their vacations. "We miss our cats big time," Rose said, "and we miss our own bed!"

Do I Need to Rent Out My Property When I am Not There to Offset Costs?

The amount of time you spend in your Mexican home will determine if it is beneficial to consider renting. If you plan on using your home for more than six months out of the year, it may not be logical for you to consider renting, as it may be difficult to secure short-term renters. Renting your property out every six months can also become a headache.

If, however, your property will be vacant for more than six months a year, it is very wise to consider taking the renting road. Although income generated by rental properties is subject to an average 25 percent tax, renting will still generate significant revenue and keep your cash flow moving. Especially if you are considering purchasing property as a second or vacation home, renting is a good option.

If you are considering renting your property — and you will not be in the country for an extended period of time to act as property manager to your renters — you will want to consider hiring someone to help you manage your property. It is nearly impossible to manage rental properties from 3,000 miles away, and the relatively small percentage of your profit that it will cost you will most likely prove well-worth it.

Do I Need to Sell My Current Home to Finance My Mexican Purchase?

It is important to consider your Mexican purchase an investment above all else. Many people become so wrapped up in the idea of owning a beach home or condo in an appealing resort, but some do not consider the financial responsibilities that owning a vacation home brings. Ask yourself if it is financially responsible for you to purchase a second home. While the appreciation of the home over, say, the next ten years may yield you a nice profit, you also have to consider the financials of funding the purchase within those ten years.

Selling a home and buying a new one simultaneously can be extremely stressful, as well as financially draining. Especially in a buyer's market, selling a home can be quite a task. If you need to use cash from the sale of your home before you can buy property in Mexico, it is wise to begin the process of selling your existing home first, and then approaching the process of buying in Mexico. Buying property in a foreign country requires a big commitment from you during the process, and it is best if you are able to be in Mexico during the entire investment process.

If you need to sell your current home in order to buy a home in Mexico, you most likely are considering moving there full-time, unless you plan to purchase in Mexico and rent a primary residence in your home country. Either way, keep in mind that unless you are paying with cash, almost all mortgage companies require a minimum of 20 percent down to finance a mortgage. Many people, particularly retirees looking to unload their primary residence and retire to Mexico, sell their home in the United States and use the profit from their sale to purchase in Mexico.

What Taxes Are Associated with a Mexican Property?

When it comes to taxes, determining your obligations is fairly straightforward. Especially if you do not plan to rent and if you will not be generating an income in Mexico, your tax obligations will not be that complicated. The tax treaty between the United States and Mexico is beneficial for Mexican property owners because it prevents double taxation on some taxes. For instance, the capital gains tax cannot be charged twice for a residence in the U.S. and Mexico; it is only charged on the property determined as your secondary residence. Mortgage interest on a Mexican property may also be also tax deductible, and if you are a U.S. citizen permanently residing in Mexico, you can pay taxes on your worldwide income instead of paying each government taxes on each income. The treaty provides even more incentive for property ownership in Mexico.

Acquisitions Tax

The acquisitions tax is also referred to as the transfer tax, and you will be required to pay this when you close on your purchase. Currently, the rate is 2 percent of your property's sale price, but it is a government rate and can change.

Property Taxes

Property taxes vary depending on which state of Mexico your property is located. Each state assesses the value of each plot of land and determines a general rate from which property taxes are calculated. The government uses this appraised rate and multiplies it by the size of your land in meters to determine the cost of your property taxes each year.

In almost every state of Mexico, property taxes are very low and add up to less than 1 percent of the value of your property per year. This usually translates to a couple hundred dollars a year.

Rental Income Tax

While property taxes remain low in Mexico, tax on rental income can be high. You will be required to pay taxes on any income you receive from renting out your Mexican property. You will be required to file tax declarations on a monthly basis.

Capital Gains Tax

Because of the tax treaty between Mexico and the United States, you will not be taxed on the profit you make on the sale of a primary residence. The tax break — $250,000 for an individual and $500,000 for married couples — was actually not intended for foreign investors; it was an incentive, as it is in the U.S., for Mexican nationals to purchase property in the country. However, if you can prove that your Mexican residence is your primary residence, and if you are a tax resident of Mexico, you can avoid paying the capital gains tax. You will have to pay capital gains if you sell your home in the U.S., considered your secondary residence in the eyes of the government if you have a primary residence in Mexico.

If you do not qualify for the tax break, you will be required to pay either 28 percent of the net gain from the sale or 25 percent of the gross revenue; the choice is yours as the seller. You will naturally want to choose the least expensive method. .

What Will It Cost Me to Live in Mexico and Run My Home?

Mexican living can be much less costly than the cost of living in the United States, but it all depends on the lifestyle you plan to lead in Mexico. In the more populated, tourist-driven areas like Los Cabos, Puerto Vallarta, and San Miguel, you can expect to pay inflated prices for almost everything. As a result from the tourism, many of these areas have been Americanized and have seen an influx of Costco Wholesales, Walmarts, and Starbucks Coffee companies.

In fact, many things are more affordable in Mexico. Some examples you will save on are:

- **Labor.** The average labor cost for home repairs and improvements, landscaping, and even nanny and housekeeper services are significantly lower than in the United States. Typically, and depending on the nature of the service, the cost of labor is lower than $5 an hour.

- **Medical care.** Compared to the exorbitant cost of health care in the United States, Mexican clinics and medical services are drastically less. Although the cost of care varies, in general you can expect to pay 25 to 50 percent less on medical and dental care in Mexico than you would in the United States. Expect to pay up to 70 percent less on prescriptions.

- **Food.** Food, particularly fruits and vegetables grown locally in Mexico, are very affordable. You will pay more for imported foods, just like any other country, but if you shop at local food and fruit stands, you will save tremendously on food. The cost of an avocado, for example, can be as much as $2.50 in some areas of the United States, but in Mexico, it is as little as 10 cents at a roadside stand.

- **Heating and cooling.** With temperatures averaging 70-80 degrees year round in many areas, you will certainly save on heating and cooling your home. The cost of electricity in Mexico is relatively high, but savings on heating and cooling will result from limited usage — not from inexpensive supply.

- **Property Taxes.** As previously mentioned, property taxes in Mexico are very low (usually less than 1 percent of the value of your property). As a comparison, you can expect to pay no more than a few hundred dollars a year for property taxes in Mexico in many areas; in some areas of New York, property taxes are more than $15,000 annually, depending on the size and location of your property.

Additionally, you will want to purchase homeowner's insurance, which is relative to the cost of insurance on your home in the United States. A typical homeowner's insurance policy will cover damage to your property from things like fire and hurricanes. Because parts of Mexico are subject to flooding at certain times of the year, it is wise to consider opting for flood damage coverage, along with earthquake coverage, which is not included in a basic policy. There are a variety of insurance companies in Mexico that cater specifically to foreign homeowners, including AIG and ING, which offer specific coverage for Mexican properties.

You will also have to take into consideration the cost of traveling to and from Mexico if you plan on using your property for only part of the year. Many airlines have picked up on the fact that so many Americans are buying real estate in Mexico, and they offer deals and affordable fares to places like Mexico City and Los Cabos.

PART II

Beginning
Your Search

CHAPTER 4

Top 15 Mexican
Real Estate Markets

O nce you have decided that buying property in Mexico is right for you, the next step is choosing a location. With so many options and so many beautiful, alluring places to select from, how do you know where to start? First, it is best to narrow down what kind of property you are looking for and what your budget is. Although the cost of property, especially beachfront, is relatively low compared to say, California, you can still expect to pay significantly more for a condo, timeshare, single-family home, or plot of land in the larger, more populated and developed communities of Mexico.

Mexico has deep historical roots; Native American tribes originally inhabited many of the towns and cities that line its shores and wind through its mountains; later, the Spaniards took over when they came to Mexico in search of new land and routes to Asia. Part of the draw to Mexico is the preserved culture and history that much of the country flaunts, and the unique opportunity to step back in time and submerge yourself in all the cultural nuances that still exist today.

The dynamics of Mexican terrain are vast, and while almost half is oceanfront, there is also an abundance of property in the mountains, desert, and forest. Surrounded by many different bodies of water, each town, city, and geographical area of Mexico has something unique to offer. As Mexico is really a developing country when it comes to real estate, there are many smaller towns and villages that are virtually untouched by developers. Here, the adventurous investor may stumble on a one-of-a-kind beachfront property for a great deal.

Until recently, for instance, much of Baja and Rosarito remained undeveloped, with valuable oceanfront plots of land undeveloped. As the demand for property has increased dramatically over the past decade and beyond, however, developers are working more quickly to put up high-rise condo developments and timeshare units along Mexico's winding coasts. If you are hoping to stumble upon a beachfront villa in a little-known town, you had better get moving.

The real estate boom that Mexico has enjoyed for the past three decades, and the past few years especially, has been partially a result of a push from Mexico's tourism promotion fund, *Fondo Nacional de Fomento al Turismo* (FONATUR). More than 30 years ago, Mexico's government formed FONATUR to boost foreign interest in Mexico to increase capital and the economy, and to create clusters of widely developed areas.

When FONATUR was initiated, the tourism agency concentrated on nurturing and building some of the county's most pristine coastline communities like Cancun, Ixtapa, and Los Cabos. It has since expanded into areas including Huatulco and Loreto and to projects including massive marinas, golf courses, theme parks, and museums. The push to lure foreign investors to Mexico's beaches continues full-steam ahead today, as the agency has many current plans underway to build on valuable land near Puerto Vallarta, Cancun, and Baja that remains relatively underdeveloped.

**QUESTIONS TO ASK YOURSELF
WHEN CONSIDERING YOUR LOCATION**

- Am I purchasing property primarily as an investment, a vacation home, a rental property, a retirement home, or a primary residence?

- Is the location in a tourist-driven or an up-and-coming area?

- How easy is it to travel to this location?

- How easy is access to medical care, shopping centers, restaurants, and beaches?

Consequently, the most popular properties amongst foreign investors are beachfront, simply because many investors purchase homes in Mexico for vacation purposes. Within the category of beachfront property, there are many different areas of Mexico, and the area you choose will determine the cost of your property. In the more developed areas of Cancun, Los Cabos, and Puerto Vallarta, you can expect to find higher property prices than some of the smaller beach towns along Mexico's coasts.

According to Matthew A. Miller of ConfiCasa Mortgage International, the three strongest real estate markets are Los Cabos, Cancun, and Puerto Vallarta. Although areas like Baja North and Puerto Penasco remain strong, "they are overbuilt and they are tied to the Arizona and California markets," he said. Still, there is much opportunity to find a great investment in areas like these, particularly considering that developers are eager to sell their properties.

Listed below are 15 areas of Mexico that are popular amongst American investors for their aesthetic beauty, varied housing options, and their potential appreciation value in today's market. This list is by no means exclusive, as there are many other communities and cities that are seeing tremendous growth and offer a wealth of opportunities to investors. For now, these are areas with growing real estate markets and plans for future development. Areas like these that have seen a solid increasing growth for a long period of time are the smartest to consider when looking for an investment.

A few of these areas, including Los Cabo, Cancun, and Puerto Vallarta, have been tourist destinations for vacationers and investors alike for many years and have proved to be wise investment choices for many foreign buyers. They are included on this list because they remain a popular choice among investors, and the value of property in these areas continues to increase. Although property in areas like Los Cabos can be just as expensive as beachfront property in California, it remains an affordable investment for many. A few of the other areas on this list, like San Carlos, Manzanillo, and San Miguel, are up-and-coming areas that have begun to see more growth in the past handful of years.

Lastly, there should be mention that many of the areas included on this list have large "gringo," or American, populations. If you are looking for a more discreet area, there are a number of cities, including Los Barriles and Cuernavaca, that offer a more authentic atmosphere. This list includes the most popular Mexican areas

— in no particular order — among foreigners, as well as up-and-coming areas in smaller towns.

1. Los Cabos

If you have ever been to Los Cabos, it is easy to understand the draw to this gorgeous beach resort area that hugs the tip of the Baja Peninsula. Vacationers have flocked to Cabo San Lucas, one of Los Cabos' towns, for many years. With opportunities to deep-sea fish, scuba dive, and golf with some of the most beautiful views in the world, the opportunities for fun, relaxation, and even retirement are endless.

One of FONATUR's initial development projects, Los Cabos comprises five main towns that stretch along the shorelines: East Cape, San Jose del Cabo, The Corridor, The Pacific, and Cabo San Lucas. While Cabo San Lucas is probably the most well-known area of Los Cabos — and consequently the most expensive — other areas like San Jose del Cabo are seeing progressive development and interest from foreign investors. Much of the land in San Jose del Cabo and East Cape in particular remains undeveloped, and opportunities for investment in one of Los Cabos' smaller towns remain abundant. Areas like these are more authentic as well, and offer investors the opportunity to live around a main hub and enjoy access to all the amenities while enjoying lower prices and a quieter neighborhood.

Los Cabos is surrounded by some of the most beautiful waters in Mexico, as the Pacific Ocean meets the Sea of Cortez to create a crystal blue sea of serenity. Given the geography of Los Cabos and its location within a peninsula, the water tends to get rough in areas of Los Cabos, which attracts surfers from around the world. In addition to the ideal surfing conditions, Los Cabos is known for its luxurious resorts, five-star restaurants, access to every water sport you can imagine, and of course, its sunsets.

Like most towns in Mexico, the history of Los Cabos dates back centuries. Its beaches and villages were once traveled on and inhabited in the 1500s by Spanish merchants who used the accessibility of Mexico's geography to trade goods with Asia and other parts of the world. Los Cabos remained relatively undeveloped until fairly recently, when infrastructure enabled easier access to its towns and beaches. Although the area is highly populated today with tourists, retirees, and vacationers, Los Cabos has retained much of its history and historic buildings, including the Old Jesuit Mission and a variety of churches.

The popularity of Los Cabos, coupled with the demand for more properties and condo developments, has encouraged developers to expand outside the limits of Los Cabos. Today, investors can find a diversity of beachfront condominium developments and timeshares that — thanks to demand from investors — will only continue to increase.

CASE STUDY: "I FELL IN LOVE WITH MEXICO"

In 1970, Linda Neil was living in the United States with her husband and two small children. With the Vietnam War and the country in a state of transition and divide, Neil and her family were looking to live an easier, better life. "People just weren't happy here," she said. "I thought 'I just don't want to be here,' and so we packed up everything, and we moved to Mexico."

Initially, the transition was hard in particular for her two small children, who found learning a new language and going to school in a foreign country quite challenging. With a real estate background and the desire to purchase property in Mexico both for personal use and as a financial investment, the Neils moved to Manzanillo, where they bought a sold a number of properties. "Real estate is in our blood!" she said.

After Manzanillo, the Neil and her family moved to Uruapan, a city in the central part of Mexico in the state of Michoacán. "It is a fascinating place," Neil said, "I love it for the Indian culture; there is no expatriate community there."

When the Neils moved to Mexico in 1970, very few of the existing laws that regulated foreign investment in real estate were established. "There was no real estate trust until 1972," she said. "So there was no way for a foreigner to buy property in the restricted zone. But outside the restricted zone, we could buy and sell."

In 1991, Neil formed The Settlement Company®, a consultancy firm that specializes in closing and escrow services, title transfer, and insurance for Mexican real estate purchases, with offices in La Paz, near Los Cabos. She saw the dire need for title insurance and escrow services in the country to protect foreign buyers, as interest began to boom. "I was a developer by trade, and I wanted to buy property, but there was no title insurance, no one to hold my money, no safeguards," she said.

Neil formed the company nearly 20 years ago and has seen tremendous growth ever since. She never anticipated her business would grow to be what it is today or that she would still even be in business. "I figured a couple of years [I'd do this], and then I could go out and play with property — not so!" she laughed. "More Americans come to Mexico, and they want the services we offer."

Although living in a foreign country was a challenging adjustment at times, Neil now lives an active lifestyle and spends her leisure time with friends and family in her La Paz condo and her mountain home in Uruapan. Her children eventually adjusted to life in Mexico, and today are grateful for the benefit of

CASE STUDY: "I FELL IN LOVE WITH MEXICO"

growing up in a diverse country and for being bilingual. Both her children married Mexican nationals, and her son now works as an education textbook translator.

Today, Neil said, buying real estate "is easy to do!" Because of her business, Neil has a sharp eye for areas that are up and coming in Mexico. She says among many areas like Puerto Vallarta, foreign buyers are interested in areas like Morelia, a small historical city in the state of Michoacán that boasts a rich history and cultural activities, along with fascinating Spanish architecture. She also noted how the crash of the U.S. housing market in 2008 affected the number of foreigners buying second, vacation, and retirement homes in Mexico. In 2008 "we lost half the market for the U.S. and Canadian buyer because they lost money in the stock market. People were taking out equity and using the cash for property in Mexico," she said.

Despite the setbacks of the recession and the ultimate hit to the Mexican real estate industry, the market is bouncing back quickly. Outside of the slower market, Neil said investing in real estate in Mexico is a great opportunity. Buyers are offered much more protection than they were 30 years ago, and that, coupled with the low real estate prices in many areas of the country, makes Mexico such an attractive place to live.

When she first came to Mexico more than 30 years ago, "I fell in love with the country" said Neil, and she has not looked back since.

Visit The Settlement Company at **www.settlement-co.com**.

2. Cancun/Playa del Carmen

If you can you leave your impression of Cancun as a spring break haven for college students behind, you will see the many opportunities this beautiful beach town offers for investors looking for a relaxing beachfront lifestyle. Located on the shores of the Gulf of Mexico, Cancun and its surrounding towns and villages have been an appealing destination for investors for many years. Its popularity has paved the way for easy access from almost anywhere in the U.S. by air to the Cancun International Airport, and much of the area has been developed to meet the needs and demands of foreigners. For many people who spend time in Cancun, it is, in essence, a home away from home.

Cancun, rich in Mayan heritage that is preserved today, was one of the first areas of Mexico to be developed to encourage tourism and travel. In the 1970s the government, through a tourism agency that later became FONATUR, created the Cancun Project to develop the area and draw tourists and vacationers from around the world. Part of the plan involved creating a variety of developments and gated communities, many of which cater to people who live in Cancun year round. Thanks to the plan, Cancun is now one of the largest cities in Mexico, with its own infrastructure, sewage, and electricity systems, water filtration system, hospitals, schools, and an international airport. Like Cabo San Lucas, there are a variety of different areas of Cancun that each offer something unique. Many of the beach towns that surround Cancun, including Playa del Carmen, Isla Mujeres, and Merida, are less populated by tourists than Cancun itself.

Similar to Los Cabos, developers are beginning to push out of the city limits of Cancun and build in these cities, particularly Playa del Carmen. Investors are attracted to places like this because they are often less populated and less expensive, but still close enough to the airport, hospitals, restaurants, and water sports. Playa del Carmen has nearly surpassed Cancun in real estate prices, most likely because of the limited amount of property in the area. Playa is slightly more diverse than Cancun, and you can find a variety of people here from college students to retirees. Although the area is more of a vacation spot than a permanent residence, there is still a strong foreigner community of permanent residents.

Even though Cancun has been popular amongst investors since the 1980s and 1990s, the area is still seeing tremendous growth. Matthew A. Miller of ConfiCasa Mortgage International has noticed an expansion of development in the area, and noted, for example, that five years ago, there was little development across the highway that cuts through Cancun. Today, developments are popping up on the outskirts of Cancun, and they are expected to continue to spread further beyond the center of this beautiful beach town in the near future. According to **www.cancun.info**, the highly anticipated Puerto Cancun is in development, which will offer a large marina and a series of hotels.

3. San Carlos

Nestled on the Sea of Cortez in the state of Sonora, San Carlos is a smaller, quieter seaside village that has seen a rapid increase in tourist and investor activity in the past few years. Perhaps for its water sports, championship golf courses, or native Mexican restaurants that dot the crevices of the San Carlos shoreline, San Carlos is considered by more Americans now for retirement and investment than ever before.

San Carlos has changed dramatically since it was first inhabited by the Guaymenas Indian tribe in the late 18th century and was used primarily as a port for trading during the Mexican-American War. Today, its valuable location puts it on the map as one of the largest commercial fishing areas in the country. Unlike some of the other densely populated tourist areas, San Carlos retains a strong local vibe and a sense of small town community. On the outskirts of San Carlos, away from the bustle of the thriving fishing and water sport community, you will find pockets of the native Guaymenas Indian villages.

Although San Carlos was first inhabited more than three centuries ago, most of it eventually became *ejidal* land meant for local peasants and their families to live on and farm. In the 1960s, the government converted San Carlos and some additional areas to private land, enabling developers to build on and investors to buy. Like Cancun, San Carlos became part of the project to increase tourism and development in the area.

The preserved culture mixed with the access to all the amenities of a large city has drawn a large population of retirees over the years. The low-key lifestyle and relative affordability of real estate in the San Carlos area makes for an ideal retirement location. In addition to single-family homes, many retirees have flocked to the various gated communities and condo and town house developments that offer privacy and luxury at an affordable price. A 250-mile drive from some areas of Arizona, San Carlos is already a hot spot for retirees from that area in particular, as well as many Mexican nationals who own vacation homes. The area therefore boasts a large English-speaking community.

While tourism and real estate investment in San Carlos has increased recently, the natives remain committed to preserving the natural resources that surround the city. The Islands of San Carlos Project aims to preserve and protect the land and waters of San Carlos by developing fishing and boating guidelines.

4. Puerto Vallarta

About halfway down the coast of the Pacific, you will find the ocean-front city of Puerto Vallarta. Surrounded by tranquil, turquoise-blue waters, Puerto Vallarta has been a vacationer's dream for decades, not to mention one of the most active real estate markets in Mexico.

Originally explored by the Spaniards in the 1500s, Puerto Vallarta saw many different phases and eventually became one of the most sought-after vacation spots in the world.

It is a dynamic and culturally enriching seaside city with lots to see, do, and enjoy. In addition to the typical beachside activities like sailing, snorkeling, and diving, Puerto Vallarta boasts an eclectic mix of history and modern culture. Art galleries, concert halls, cultural festivals, and the Los Arcos National Marine Park are just some of the things to keep you entertained in Puerto Vallarta. The main hub offers more than 200 restaurants, a variety of five-star hotels and bed and breakfasts, as well as entertainment and shopping. Visitors and vacationers also find traveling to Puerto Vallarta easy, as the airport is less than five miles from the center of town. People also enjoy the relative proximity to other popular areas of Mexico, like Mazatlán and Guadalajara.

Foreign interest in Puerto Vallarta dates back centuries when the small seaside village was used for harboring fishing boats and transporting goods in and out of the country. Interest in Puerto Vallarta as a vacation and tourist destination dates back to the early 1900s, after which the area saw a large boom in development that has continued ever since.

Although the project was not part of FONATUR's initial development plan to draw tourism to Mexico, the agency has a number of planned development projects in the surrounding areas of Puerto Vallarta, which include condo developments, shopping centers, marinas, golf courses, and more. The entire development will be high-end and geared toward the more aggressive investor.

The diverse dynamic of Puerto Vallarta has attracted investors looking for a high profile, luxurious, beachfront community with an international flare. With tourism touted as one of the main industries, Puerto Vallarta is similar to Cancun and Los Cabos in terms of tourism, prices, and availability of real estate. The diversity of real estate available in Puerto Vallarta makes it appealing to investors of all kinds, whether you are looking for a one-bedroom condo in the center of town or a four-bedroom villa with an ocean view.

CASE STUDY: FROM CANADA TO MEXICO

In 2007, native Canadian Michael Murphy made the move from Vancouver Island to Mexico to enjoy a more laidback way of life. Settling in a small city outside of Puerto Vallarta, Murphy chose Bucerías for its idealistic climate, white sandy beaches, affordable health care, and easy-living lifestyle. "When it comes to language, to the way of doing thing in Mexico, certainly the word '*mañana*' comes to mind," Murphy said. "*Mañana* does not mean tomorrow, it means 'No, I can't do it tomorrow!' "

Although it can take a bit of time to get things done in Bucerías, Murphy enjoys the lifestyle. He enjoys the people and the culture, access to many amenities like great restaurants, and a much cheaper way of life.

Murphy and his wife Clara decided to move to Mexico a few years ago after more than two decades in the real estate business. With his daughter and grandchildren already living in Bucerías, they decided to follow suit and buy a second home in the area. They purchased a condo in a nice development just a few blocks from the beach. His development boasts a pool, beautiful landscaping and gardening, and security. The best part is the low maintenance fee — around $100 a month — which makes it very affordable for the Murphys to enjoy their second home.

The Murphys, accustomed to the cool temperatures of Vancouver Island, spend the warm summer months in Canada, where they still own several properties. By March, they are headed south to their home in Bucerías. As a real estate professional, Murphy established Bienvenidos Real Estate, a successful real estate company that specializes in property in the Puerto Vallarta area.

Whether he is north or south of the border, Murphy enjoys the luxury of being able to work from both his homes. As an active professional in the real estate

CASE STUDY: FROM CANADA TO MEXICO

industry, Murphy works with a lot of Canadians and Americans who are interested in purchasing real estate in Mexico. He enjoys guiding foreigners through the process and helping them navigate the intricacies of the real estate system, which includes avoiding unscrupulous real estate agents and other professionals. When Murphy founded the company, he said, he "hit the ground running" and has seen a tremendous demand for his services.

Although many foreigners come to Mexico to retire and buy second homes, there are a growing number of young people buying homes in Bucerías as well. The mixture of generations provides a diverse and intrinsic population while still maintaining its culture and charm.

With shopping, dining, medical care, easy access to the airport, and pristine sandy beaches, Bucerías is proving to be a more popular retirement and vacation destination for foreigners from around the world. The small fishing village, whose name means "Place of the Divers," has seen an expansion of amenities to meet the demand of the increasing foreign population. Recently, a new mega store similar to Walmart was built in the area, providing a great opportunity to purchase affordable food, clothes, household items, and other amenities.

His advice to others considering purchasing property and moving to Mexico is simple: "If it's your first venture down [to Mexico], it's best to go down and try it first," Murphy said. "Go down and rent, spend three to six months there. I would not recommend, for the most part, that people try to go down there and buy something quick."

When it comes to his work as a real estate agent, Murphy believes in being honest with buyers. "It comes back to human relationships," he said. "People can tell if you are giving them the straight goods, taking time to educate them, and looking out for their best interest." And he ensures that he does just that when he is helping clients find the perfect home.

As far as adapting, Murphy says a little courtesy goes a long way. "People are friendly for the most part, as long as you remember you are putting yourself in a different culture," he said. "The onus is on us to learn the different ways of culture, not to impose our ways on them. Again, it comes back to common mutual respect. Just remember the Golden Rule and respect the way other cultures do things. If you are from out of town, you need to be a learner and a listener, and not someone that is dictating and expecting things to be done."

Visit Bienvenidos Real Estate at **www.bienvenidosrealestate.com**.

5. Manzanillo

Unlike the populated, Americanized Los Cabos and Cancun, Manzanillo is a low-key, laidback city that boasts beautiful beaches that stretch for miles, a thriving fishing industry, and an array of natural wonders. Nestled between El Fuego and El Nevado volcanoes, Manzanillo is more of an off-the-beaten-path type with rich culture and a diverse cultural dynamic.

Manzanillo boasts some of the best-known and most challenging golf courses, including Isla Navidad, La Mantarraya at Las Hadas Golf Resort and Marina, and El Tamarindo Resort. The city is also big on sport fishing and hosts a variety of tournaments each year that draw enthusiasts from around the world. In addition to the typical water sports like snorkeling, sailing, and diving, Manzanillo offers beautiful hiking trails and whale-watching excursions, as well as biking tours through the mountainous terrain that serves as the city's picturesque backdrop.

Manzanillo served as a harbor for Hernán Cortés in the late 1500s and later became an important trading seaport for successions of explorers. In the early 1900s, the Mexican government contributed to Manzanillo's growth by funneling money into projects to develop the city's infrastructure and operating systems. Today, Manzanillo is a popular stop for cruising vessels and wandering sailors alike.

Manzanillo has maintained its historical roots over the years and many travelers to this small community on the Mexican Riviera enjoy the preserved culture and native flare that vibrate through the city. Unlike some of the higher-end communities along Mexico's beaches and inland, Manzanillo is a family-friendly vacation spot and offers many activities that younger visitors enjoy.

Probably less glamorous than some of the well-known development cities like Cancun and Los Cabos, Manzanillo is the perfect spot to find a cozy beach bungalow by the sea or hidden amongst the city's dynamic and lush landscape. Despite its low-key atmosphere, there are all kinds of property available in Manzanillo from seaside villas, luxury condos, and gated communities that boast five-star amenities. Retirees and investors looking for a quiet beach vacation have flocked to Manzanillo to find affordable housing options in a beautiful, laidback, friendly atmosphere.

6. Mazatlán

Mazatlán is a smaller beach city along Mexico's Gold Coast that is touted as the "Pearl of the Pacific." With sprawling beaches that stretch for miles, sparkling blue waters, and rich terrain, Mazatlán is an attractive spot for foreign buyers looking for a relaxed atmosphere and an affordable investment that will turn a nice profit down the line. In fact, this city is one of the most affordable beach towns in the entire country.

A big draw to Mazatlán is the variety of things to do and places to see. The vast tourist district known as the Zona Dorada offers a plethora of activities and events that appeal to a diversity of people. The islands of Chivos, Venados, and Pajaros, in addition to Punta Camaron, offer Mazatlán's visitors a diversity of terrain to explore and plush scenery to enjoy. The surrounding desert terrain provides a beautiful backdrop to the bustle of Mazatlán's central plaza, where you can find a native food market, unique shops, and delicious restaurants.

Although Native American tribes initially inhabited Mazatlán, Spaniards later took control in the early 1500s. Its biggest growth period occurred at the turn of the century, and more so during the 1960s, when tourists began to flock to the area to relax and vacation. Since then, Mazatlán has seen much growth in the form of high-rise hotels and other tourist attractions but has maintained much of its rich history and culture. The Basílica de la Purísima Concepción is just one of the historical attractions that the city offers.

Despite the more secluded nature of Mazatlán, the city offers a variety of resort and condo developments, which offer some of the most beautiful properties in close proximity to the beach. The resorts also boast beautiful golf courses in a private yet luxurious setting. Because of Mazatlán's jagged geography, much of the real estate is not directly on the beach, but very close to it. The variety of terrain in Mazatlán appeals to investors looking for a little diversity while remaining unwilling to sacrifice all the amenities of a larger city. There is an international airport nearby and a strong English-speaking community.

7. San Miguel

San Miguel is the most artistic and culturally diverse city on this list. The variety of foreigners that reside in San Miguel, located in the mountains of Guanajuato, make the city right with international and creative flare. The variety of academic institutions in San Miguel, including the *Academia Hispano Americana* and the *Instituto Allende*, contribute to its cultural diversity and European feel.

While there is a high population of Americans and therefore an English-speaking community, you will find San Miguel to be more authentic than places like Mazatlán, Los Cabos, and Cancun. San Miguel has remained loyal to its cultural and historical roots and the city itself is an historical landmark, preserving many original colonial buildings and cobblestone streets. Some of the original remains of buildings and other structures that date back to 900 A.D. remain in the city and now sit on preserved sites.

San Miguel was originally founded in the 1500s, when Franciscan monk Juan de San Miguel chose the area to settle and pursue his religious missions. It was later occupied by military forces and was eventually named San Miguel de Allende for Ignacio Allende, a captain of the Spanish army who contributed to the defense of Mexico's freedom from Spain.

Given San Miguel's location in central Mexico, it is not a beach town. But there are top-notch restaurants, hotels, festivals, art galleries, cooking classes, and of course, the centuries-old architecture to enjoy. Many visitors and locals alike frequent the charming cafes that line the city's cobblestone streets and enjoy the city's mild climate year round. Taboada hot springs is also a big attraction.

San Miguel is not the easiest place to get to if you are traveling by air; the closet international airport is about 70 miles from the mountainous village. Many transportation companies, however, offer affordable shuttle service to and from the airports.

There are a variety of options when it comes to real estate in San Miguel, as it offers single-family homes and villas within the city, as well as condo and housing developments in gated communities right outside the city limits. There is also undeveloped land for sale on the outskirts of the city that will undoubtedly prove a beautiful location for a custom-built home. Be aware that in general, real estate is more expensive in San Miguel than many other areas of Mexico and caters to a high-end buyer.

8. Huatulco

Huatulco is located on the Pacific coast of Mexico, way down south in the state of Oaxaca. Although tourism is increasing to this once-secluded nook on Mexico's coastline, the area remains an ideal vacation and retirement spot for investors looking for a more natural and rugged location.

The best known attraction in Huatulco are the nine bays that snake in and out of the city's coastline: Conejos, Chahue, Tangolunda, Santa Cruz, Playa San Augustin, Cacaluta, Maguey, Chachacual, and the Playa Organo. The beautiful blue waters that form the nine bays serve as ideal swimming, snorkeling, diving, and sailing locations in a secluded and private atmosphere. Many visitors and locals love the rugged and undeveloped terrain of Huatulco and all the adventures the land offers.

Pirates and passers-by first inhabited Huatulco centuries ago; they used the ideal location to transport goods and fish the waters. Compared to other developed areas of Mexico, Huatulco is fairly young and, thanks to FONATUR, has emerged from the days of a secluded seaside village to a hot spot for foreign vacationers and investors. The tourism agency has a plan to create a large marina in the bays of Huatulco that will be able to house cruise ships and other large boats, as well as a vast shopping mall, new restaurants, and condominium developments.

In addition to bike paths, horseback riding, and hiking, you will find ample opportunity to shop, dine, go to the theatre, and discover handmade wood art crafted by the indigenous people of the area. Although Playa Santa Cruz is the best-known beach in town, Huatulco's nine bays offer a number of ultra private beaches, as many of them are only accessible by boat. Thanks in part to the *Parque Nacional Huatulco*, many of the secluded beaches that make up the city's coastline remain protected and undeveloped.

As far as real estate goes, investors and vacationers have a variety of options. Condo developments, secluded and oceanfront villas, and bed and breakfasts line the shores of Huatulco offering every kind of visitor the chance to enjoy the city's natural beauty. FONATUR is in the process of building the area up, and developers are building condo developments, timeshares, and town houses along the sandy shores of Huatulco. Because the area is relatively new, investing now would be wise, as you will be able to find a good deal on properties.

9. Loreto

Located on the Sea of Cortez coast in the state of Baja California, Loreto is a prominent fishing and sailing location that offers an abundance of activities and nuances for every type of visitor. Surrounded by desert, sea, and mountains, Loreto boasts a wide range of things to do including snorkeling, diving, golfing, hiking, biking, and exploring. It is no wonder Jacques Cousteau called Loreto his favorite tropical paradise.

Loreto has preserved much of its cultural heritage, and visitors revel in the explorations of old missions, including the mission church Our Lady of Loreto, nestled in the mountains of San Javier, a close ride from downtown Loreto. The caves that contour the mountains surrounding Loreto have some of the oldest and most fascinating cave drawings that offer a glimpse into Loreto's flavored history.

Back in the center of town, many of Loreto's restaurants reflect its culture, offering traditional Mexican cuisine in an authentic yet upscale atmosphere. High-end accommodations like The Resort at Loreto Bay offer luxurious, five-star amenities and attract visitors from around the world. The city also boasts the Loreto Bay National Marine Park, a UNESCO World Heritage Site that is home to many species of whales and other exotic oceanic creatures.

You will begin to hear more about Loreto in the coming year, as it is one of FONATUR's latest development areas. The tourism agency has big plans for Loreto, which include low-rise condo developments, villa communities, restaurants, low-key shopping centers, and golf and spa resorts, many of which are already built. The agency remains committed to keeping the development eco-friendly and to maintaining a sense of authenticity and culture to the area. Like many other up-and-coming spots in Mexico, Loreto has its own international airport, enabling convenient travel to and from the rest of the world.

There are a variety of real estate options in Loreto, and the opportunities for investment are on the rise. Timeshares, condo developments, and raw plots of land can be pricey in this seaside city, but if you can still find a good deal, as the area is still relatively undiscovered and is in the process of being developed. Loreto real estate prices remain significantly lower than prices in places like Los Cabos and Cancun, which makes it a great market for its idealistic and aesthetic location.

10. Zihuatanejo-Ixtapa

You can find Ixtapa and Zihuatanejo on Mexico's Pacific Coast, north of Acapulco. With blue waters and white beaches that stretch for more than eight miles, Zihuatanejo is a vacationer's paradise and a retiree's dream. Investors have eyed Zihuatanejo as a smart investment location for many years, as the area offers a nice blend of activities and amenities.

Zihuatanejo is a cozy town with historic roots in the Aztecs, who were eventually ousted from the area by Hernán Cortés in his explorations up the coast of Mexico. In addition to the bustle of activity and entertainment in the center of Zihuatanejo, visitors can also enjoy the various areas that extend beyond the city, including Troncones and Barra de Potosi. Troncones is a quiet village just a short trip from Zihuatanejo that offers the serenity of undeveloped terrain and secluded beaches. Similarly, Barra de Potosi is a sleepy seaside town that counts a saltwater lagoon, a wildlife sanctuary, and miles of beach as its main attractions.

Ixtapa, located about five miles from the center of Zihuatanejo, is FONATUR's extensive resort project initiated in the 1970s. With five-star amenities, Ixtapa is a world-class destination for elite vacationers from around the world. With more than ten beaches, the area has a variety of different real estate options and investment opportunities in condo developments, timeshares, and secluded homes.

Thanks to the tourism agency, Zihuatanejo has come a long way since the 1960s, when it was an isolated, little-known beach town on the edge of the Pacific Ocean. Seeing the inherent value in its location, FONATUR focused on Zihuatanejo as one of its initial projects, building roads, sewer, electricity systems, stores, restaurants, and resort communities. The area also includes its own airport, enabling easy access for travelers. Zihuatanejo has also gained some notoriety from films including *The Shawshank Redemption*, when Morgan Freeman's character mentions the unknown beach town as his idealistic retreat.

Although FONATUR pumped millions of dollars into the Zihuatanejo community many years ago, and it has since been a popular vacation destination, the area remains relatively secluded compared to the other development areas. The beaches along the shorelines offer ample opportunity to find a private spot, away from some of the hustle and bustle of the tourist activity.

11. Guadalajara

With more than three million people in this Mexican city, Guadalajara is a popular place for retirees and investors, as it offers an ideal balance between city life and tropical paradise. With access to excellent medical care, public transportation, schools, and other big-city amenities, Guadalajara has been a popular choice for retirees in particular for years.

As the second-largest city in Mexico and the origin of mariachi music and tequila, Guadalajara is an historic, international city with rich culture and a worldly flair. The city boasts some of the best restaurants in the country, as well as a variety of entertainment, traditional celebrations and festivals, and a zoo, among many other things to see and do. Additionally, golfers flock here for the beautiful courses, and country club enthusiasts enjoy the variety of clubs to join. Tennis is also a popular activity in Guadalajara among foreigners and vacationers.

Guadalajara, part of Tequila Country, is a major international city and therefore is easy to access from many places. Transportation within the city is easy, as is access to medical facilities. The city is also centrally located to several smaller cities and towns in the surrounding area, including Chapala and Ajijic. If you live near the border, Guadalajara is easily accessible by car as well.

The history of Guadalajara dates back to the 1500s, when the city was founded by a Spanish explorer and later inhabited by Spaniards. In the years that followed the Mexican Revolution, Guadalajara flourished with international activity and developed socially, industrially, and economically. It has since remained one of the most active hubs in Mexico.

There are a variety of gringo and retirement developments in Guadalajara that range in price from moderate to expensive and offer beautiful condos and single-family villas. The housing options are still reasonable, perhaps because Guadalajara offers more of a city atmosphere versus a beach community. Many retirement communities, in beautiful gated developments, are located on Lake Chapala, which offers the opportunity to live near water.

Given the idealistic weather and its big-city atmosphere, Guadalajara draws a range of different business, retirement, and vacation-minded people. The city also has a large art scene, which draws creative artistic types as well.

12. Punta Mita

Located just over 25 miles north of Puerto Vallarta on the coast of the Mexican Riviera, Punta Mita has been a well-known luxury vacation and retirement spot among foreigners for many years.

Punta Mita is in the state of Nayarit, which borders Jalisco, home state to Puerto Vallarta. The city of Punta Mita sits on a corner of the Bahia de Banderas, the largest bay in Mexico. The areas, cities, and beaches that surround Punta Mita are bursting with upscale, gated community developments, beachfront condos, private single-family villas and houses, and timeshare options. It is also possible to purchase empty lots to build your dream home.

Hugged by the Sierra Madre Mountains, the Bahia de Banderas is a beautiful, tropical paradise. With temperatures that hover around 90 degrees most of the year and a limited rainy season, the 40 miles of white beaches that surround the Bahia de Banderas are an ideal location for a vacation or retirement home. The bay itself has a rich archeological history, as it was created from an ancient volcano that erupted and left a vast, deep hole that created the Bahia de Banderas. The geography of the bay creates an ideal tropical climate, and the mountains protect the water from strong winds, creating a cool and calm surf that mirrors a vast, crystal-blue pool.

Outside the city of Punta Mita are many opportunities to explore culture, food, entertainment, and beaches. Nayarit's capital, Tepic, is a mild drive from Punta Mita and serves as a main hub as well as a large marketplace for authentic handmade crafts and artifacts. Nuevo Vallarta, a large high-end development community, is close to Punta Mita's own master-plan development that includes private beaches, golf courses, and a new, beautiful Four Seasons Hotel. The inclusion of the hotel in the development offers residents exclusive restaurants and shops as well.

Although Punta Mita is similar to Cancun and Puerto Vallarta in the context of being very developed and having a large foreigner population, new developments of condos, villas, and timeshares offer an abundance of investment options that range from moderate to very expensive. The variety of options draws a diverse number of foreigners, from high-end investors looking for a private villa in a gated community to people looking to spend a few weeks a year in Punta Mita in a small timeshare on the beach. Despite its popularity for many years, real estate has seen a boom in the last five to seven years in particular. Developments have expanded further and further each year beyond the initial Punta Mita community, bringing with them many options for foreign investors.

13. Los Barriles/Buena Vista

Los Barriles and Buena Vista are small, quaint, and unassuming fishing villages located in the state of Baja California Sur on the Baja Peninsula. Compared to areas like Punta Mita, Cancun, and Puerto Vallarta, Los Barriles and Buena Vista are seaside villages that have a limited number of foreigners year-round.

Located on the eastern coast of the Baja Peninsula, Los Barriles is not far from the five areas of Los Cabos, which is great for investors looking for easy access to larger cities and towns, as well as luxury amenities, five-star restaurants, golf courses, and medical care. The small seaside village is among many of its kind that line the eastern coast of the Peninsula and offers ideal fishing and other water sports like kite surfing, sailing, and diving. About 45 minutes from San Jose del Cabo, Los Barriles is easily accessible to the San Jose airport.

Like Los Barriles, Buena Vista offers an authentic, rustic atmosphere in a more secluded, quieter area of the coast. Located just five minutes from the center of Los Barriles, Buena Vista boasts a quiet and quaint way of life, as well as a variety of higher-end developments and opportunities to scuba dive, sail, deep-sea fish, and snorkel in pristine waters. The Sierra de La Laguna mountain range that surrounds Buena Vista offers ample opportunity to hike and mountain bike, and serves as an ideal backdrop for this seaside fishing village.

As the real estate market has seen tremendous growth in the past five to ten years, Los Barriles and Buena Vista have slowly begun to draw some attention. Most foreigners who invest here are looking for a more laidback, cultural, authentic town away from the hustle and bustle of city life and larger gringo development areas. Because the areas are not as developed, there remain many great nooks and crannies off the beaten path that provide opportunities to build or buy a dream home. While developers are starting to take interest in Los Barriles and Buena Vista and developing communities, there is still a good amount of beautiful oceanfront property and empty lots.

Many foreigners who stumble upon Los Barriles and Buena Vista and purchase property here build homes on the available beachfront property and in the bluffs overlooking the sea. Growth in these areas in particular is expected to grow tremendously as investors and developers extend outside the Los Cabos area to smaller villages that offer equally beautiful land and property for much less.

14. Queretaro

Located about three hours from Mexico City, Queretaro is a cultured, colonial, and historic town. The city has that small-town charm and serves as the capital of the state of San Miguel de Queretaro. Positioned in central Mexico, Queretaro is an easy drive to Guanajuato and Mexico City.

Queretaro is rich with history. The Spaniards originally inhabited it in the 1500s, and after the Spanish conquest, the city became an important because of its valuable location and proximity to Guanajuato and Mexico City. The Spaniards even nicknamed the Queretaro the "third city of the kingdom," which signified its importance during the Spanish rule. The city's religious significance originated during the conquest as well, when the local people were convinced to convert to Catholicism and built churches and missionaries to practice their faith. Junípero Serra, a Catholic missionary, began his travels in Queretaro, and the city has enjoyed a rich religious culture ever since.

Queretaro boasts one of the highest population growth rates out of many similar Mexican cities. Although there are a limited number of foreigners in Queretaro, it is becoming an increasingly popular area for Americans and Canadians, as it offers a cultured atmosphere in a big city with affordable housing options and a small foreign community. Many come to Queretaro to tour the beautiful architecture and churches and to enjoy the laidback atmosphere that the city offers. The city has more than 200 hotels and bed and breakfasts, as well as many top-notch and local restaurants and cafes. Because Queretaro is a big city, amenities like medical care, grocery stores, and transportation are easily accessible.

Although Queretaro is not a beach town, it has much to offer. In the downtown area, there are many historic churches and buildings that date back centuries, as well as small cafes and plazas that offer traditional Mexican music, museums, and art galleries. You can also find marketplaces to buy traditional pottery, jewelry, and ceramics.

Despite the fact that Queretaro is a big city, there are many recreational things to do and sports to enjoy such as golf and polo. On the outskirts of the city are a variety of housing options, including unique single-family homes. There are also a variety of renting options, and many foreigners who think of moving here visit the city first and even rent for a few months to get a feel for the city.

CASE STUDY: RETIRING SOUTH OF THE BORDER

In 2000, Barry Lipman was ready to think about retirement. After 30 years in New York and traveling around various parts of the world and South America, Lipman decided to investigate his piqued interest in Mexico. He had always been drawn to the country, the less expensive and laidback style of living, and the friendly people. "I had taken a trip to Guanajuato in 2000 to see about moving there; I was thinking about it," Lipman said.

In 2001, Lipman made the leap and rented a series of apartments and houses in

CASE STUDY: RETIRING SOUTH OF THE BORDER

Guanajuato to experience living in the city before deciding to buy something. "I rented for six months, which gave me time to organize things and live there," he said. Lipman traveled back and forth to the United States during that time as well. "At the end of the six months, I knew I wanted to come back," he added. And that he did.

Lipman returned to Guanajuato. "When I first moved there, I lived here and there for two-and-a-half years, and I really had no plans to buy property. I rented a few different apartments," he said. Although he loved Guanajuato, he was more drawn to Queretaro, where a friend of his lived. "Guanajuato is very picturesque; it is a very old-colonial city," Lipman said. "The terrain is hilly; the streets are on hills. I knew a friend who bought a house in Queretaro, and I visited for the weekend to check out the place and made up my mind to move there."

Lipman had always had Queretaro in the back of his mind, and he always had an inkling he wanted to live there. He found the spread out nature of the terrain in Guanajuato a little too spacious, and as a retiree, he was looking for a closer walk to town, restaurants, and entertainment. While he rented an apartment, Lipman linked up with a broker to consider buying a piece of property.

After taking a look at a number of properties in the area that just were not right, Lipman stumbled up on a "For Sale" sign while walking through town one day. "I called the woman," he said, "and the house was relatively small compared to some of the mansions in the area, but I bought the location; it has a very nice view. Most houses are one to two stories, and this one was three."

It took about nine months and some initial renovations until the house was livable. Lipman now lives full-time in his Queretaro house, which boasts indoor and outdoor living areas and is located in the center of town. "[The house] is in the historic district and faces a pedestrian street with a plaza," Lipman said. "It's the perfect central location." He now enjoys walking into town, listening to the mariachi music, visiting the local cafes, and admiring the architecture of the city's buildings and plazas. "I love the people, the language, the climate," he added.

Like most people who flock to Queretaro, Lipman touts the city's European atmosphere as a big draw. He also enjoys having access to American-based stores like Costco and Walmart, which makes grocery shopping and accessing amenities very easy. In the short time that Lipman has lived in Queretaro, he has noticed a variety of new construction and expansion projects, including commercial and residential properties. "The city is beautiful, clean, and well-kept," he said.

As for his plans for the future, Lipman plans to stay in Queretaro permanently. "This is my home; this is where I live," he said.

15. Guanajuato

This small city is located near Queretaro in the center of Mexico in the state of Guanajuato. With a seasonal climate and a small foreign community, Guanajuato is a very cultured, historic city with much to offer.

The origins of this city date back centuries. It was one of the first areas founded by the Spaniards in the 1500s and was initially recognized for its valuable mines of silver and other metals. The original architecture and buildings still exist throughout the city, as well as many churches and other historical buildings. The preservation of the city's rich heritage gives the city an authentic feel.

The city is a walking city, and most of the homes that dot the hills and cliffs throughout the city are unique and somewhat private. Real estate can be expensive, but if you take time to look close enough, or even consider renting while you search for an ideal property, you may be able to find a good deal. The heart of the city has no cars, which greatly reduces pollution and creates a more pedestrian- and tourist-friendly environment. On the other hand, it also restricts access to stores, shops, and restaurants for those who live here.

Guanajuato is well-known for its European atmosphere and artistic and creative residents, as well as its charming cobblestone streets, plazas, and squares that offer entertainment and shopping. Although housing can be on the more expensive side, prices are significantly less than San Miguel, to which Guanajuato is often compared. Like any city, the closer you live to the center of town, the more you can expect to pay for housing. If you venture to the outskirts of the city and choose a residential neighborhood bordering the center of town, you can expect to pay less for a larger, more modern living space. Given its colonial feel, many of the buildings in the center of the city are very dated and preserved, so if you are looking for something more modern, your best bet is to look outside the center of town.

For many, Guanajuato is an ideal location given its limited foreign population, its preserved European atmosphere, and its central location to the airport, medical care, grocery stores, and restaurants. The old-world charm is a big draw for many, who find Guanajuato has an ideal balance of foreigners and Mexican nationals.

Location Recap

Town/City	Pros	Cons	Ideal location for...
Cancun/ Playa Del Carmen	-Access to medical care, restaurants, nightlife, and American grocery stores -Easily accessible -Luxurious condos and amenities -Great beaches -Calm clear waters	-Very high prices -Large American/ foreign population -Very touristy and transient -Less of an authentic feel -Big vacation spot for young people	Buyers looking for luxurious oceanfront, high-rise condo developments and exclusive five star gated communities in a highly populated, tourist area with easy access to an airport, medical care, and stores like Costco and Walmart. Playa del Carmen is ideal for buyers who are looking for a more diverse area than Cancun in a smaller, more bohemian town with competing real estate prices.

Town/City	Pros	Cons	Ideal location for...
Los Cabos	-Access to medical care, restaurants, nightlife, and American grocery stores -Easily accessible -Luxurious condos and amenities -Surfer's paradise	-High to very high prices -Large American/ foreign population -Very touristy and transient -Less of an authentic feel -Rough waters that sometimes prohibit water sports	Investors looking for a luxurious, modern vacation or retirement home in beachfront, high-rise condo developments with all the amenities and access to five-star resorts, restaurants, and golf courses, and every water activity under the sun.
San Carlos	-Decent access to medical care -Drivable from the southern U.S. -Great fishing and water sports -Access to all amenities -Laid back low profile atmosphere -Beautiful seaside town	-Fairly expensive real estate -Large American/ foreign population -Can be seasonally transient	Investors looking for a less populated, more authentic, small-town seaside village with a relaxed and laidback atmosphere, access to big city amenities, and affordable town houses and condo developments in gated and seaside communities.

Town/City	Pros	Cons	Ideal location for...
Puerto Vallarta	-Decent access to medical care -Easily accessible -Cultural nightlife and restaurants -Great golfing -Varied terrain provides lots of real estate options and beautiful views	-Expensive real estate -Large American/ foreign population -Waters can be rough -Summers can be very hot -Some beaches are rocky -Hills can make driving and walking challenging	Investors looking for high-end properties in development communities and within the city with a little more of an international culture and atmosphere than Cancun and Los Cabos.
Manzanillo	-Decent access to medical care -Small town authentic feel -Affordable real estate -Varied populations -Excellent fishing and golfing -Beautiful beaches	-Limited cultural activities and restaurants, grocery stores, and other amenities -Can get touristy -Summers can be very hot	Investors looking for an off-the-beaten-path seaside city with a quiet, low-key, family-friendly atmosphere and a diversity of housing options including high-end condos and remote villas.

Town/City	Pros	Cons	Ideal location for...
Mazaltán	-Excellent access to medical care -Affordable real estate -Access to all amenities -Local feel -Variety of cultural activities and nightlife	-Large American/ foreign population -Can be touristy and crowded -Spring break spot for young people	Investors looking for affordable condos and timeshares in a beachside city with a large number of English-speaking people and tourists.
San Miguel	-Decent access to medical care -Very cultural, authentic town -Access to all amenities -Laid back, quiet, artsy atmosphere	-Expensive to very expensive real estate -Winters can be chilly -Not the easiest place to travel to -Not a beach town	Investors looking for unique, secluded villas and single-family homes within a culturally enriched city, or condo or single-family homes in a gated community on the outskirts of the city.

Town/City	Pros	Cons	Ideal location for...
Huatulco	-Beautiful beach town with undiscovered terrain -Up-and-coming area -Affordable real estate prices and varied options -Great opportunity for investment -Many beaches are protected from development	-Town is fairly secluded with limited access to amenities	Investors looking for an up-and-coming secluded beach village with an increasing tourist population, new development communities, and retail shops, restaurants, golf courses, and recreational activities on land and water.
Loreto	-Culturally diverse -Authentic feel, varied real estate options -Easily accessible -Access to amenities, restaurants, nightlife -Limited American/ foreign population	-Real estate can be expensive -Summers are very hot	Investors looking to get a good deal on property that will appreciate over time in an up and coming beachside city with easy access to airports and other amenities.

Town/City	Pros	Cons	Ideal location for...
Zihuatanejo/ Ixtapa	-Lots to do and see -Access to all amenities -Luxurious condos and resort options -Variety of beaches -Culturally diverse -Easily accessible	-Ixtapa is touristy; can be expensive	Investors looking for affordable real estate in a developed area, with access to all the amenities as well as secluded beaches, wildlife, and cultural diversity.
Guadalajara	-Limited American/foreign population -Cultured and authentic atmosphere -Excellent access to medical care and city amenities -Affordable living	-Real estate can be expensive, depending on location -Pollution, crowding, busy-city atmosphere creates less laid back feel	Investors looking for moderately priced condos and villas in development communities in a larger international city atmosphere with access to public transportation, medical care, five-star restaurants, golfing, tennis, and cultural activities.
Punta Mita	-Lots to do and see -Access to five-star amenities and restaurants -Accessible medical care -Variety of real estate options -Easily accessible	-Expensive to very expensive real estate -Increasing American/ foreign community -Can be touristy	Investors looking for a variety of moderate to very expensive condo developments, timeshares, private villas, and empty lots on beachfront property and in exclusive gated communities with access to big-city and luxurious amenities with easy access to travel, other cities, and medical care.

Town/City	Pros	Cons	Ideal location for...
Los Barriles/ Buena Vista	-Quiet beach towns -Limited foreign population -Access to Los Cabos amenities -Great fishing, sailing, hiking, and golfing -Laid-back, authentic feel	-Prices are increasing rapidly -Increasing American and foreign population	Investors looking for a smaller, quieter, more authentic seaside fishing village with a variety of condo and time-share developments, as well as raw land on the beach and in bluffs, with access to the Los Cabos area and easy access to amenities and an airport.
Queretaro	-Very cultural and international -Authentic restaurants -Old Mexico atmosphere -Small foreign community -Affordable real estate -Access to American stores and medical care -Easily accessible	-Increasing American presence -Increasing real estate prices -Not a beach town	Investors looking for a non-beach environment in a large, cultured city with rich flavor and history with easy access to medical care, transportation, airports, and a limited foreign community.
Guanajuato	-Decent access to medical care -Limited foreign population -Very cultural -Variety of real estate options	-Hilly terrain can limit walking, and driving is prohibited in the center of town -Can get crowded and touristy	Investors looking for a European-type walking city with a limited variety of housing options in a city with all the amenities and easy access to medical care and a small foreign and English-speaking community.

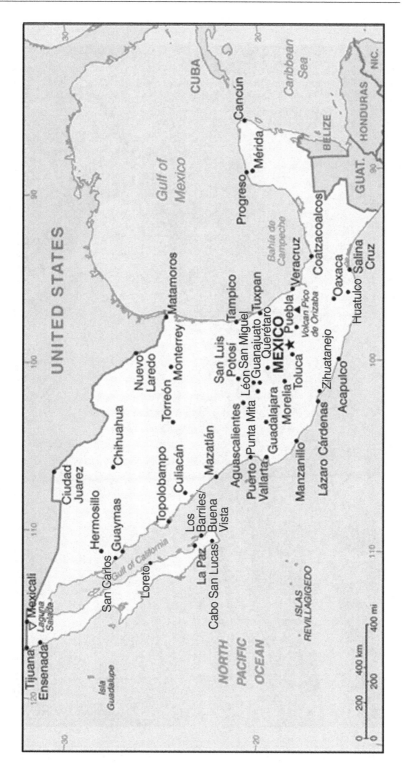

CHAPTER 5

What to Look Out For and What to Avoid

J ust as you would in any other country, you need to take a series of precautions when you purchase real estate in Mexico. After all, your purchase should be considered a financial investment in addition to a vacation or retirement home to enjoy, and you should therefore take every step necessary to ensure that your investment is secure and ultimately profitable.

It is important to also consider the process of selling your property when or if you chose to do so down the road, as you want to make sure that five years from now you have all the information and proper documents you need to sell it. If you bypass a step in the purchasing process and, say, invest in a condo in a new development and do not enlist a *notario publico* to do a proper title search, you will undoubtedly run into issues when you go to sell your condo and do not have the right title documents to pay to the new buyer.

There are a number of things you should be wary of and avoid before you even begin the process of purchasing property in Mexico.

Being aware of these things up-front will help prevent you from making a mistake along the way that may cost you valuable time and money. This chapter will outline things to avoid during the investment process, and discuss the dangers of undocumented transactions, irrevocable power of attorney, and unclear contracts.

The more you look at the big picture in regard to your purchase, the better off you will be in the end. Knowing how to navigate your way around the investment process will give you the power to make your purchase as easy, secure, and profitable as it can be. Knowing what to avoid and what *not* to do is usually a great step to learning what you *should* do.

What You Should Not Do When Purchasing Property in Mexico

1. **Give money to your real estate agent to hold in escrow.** There are no escrow companies like there are in the U.S. Giving your money to any company or person who claims to be an escrow service is highly risky unless you can confirm that the company is a legitimate escrow service. For many years, professionals have warned that if you are willing to give your money to the seller of your property — either real estate agents or a third party you have not researched and confirmed is a legitimate escrow service — you can be prepared not to get it back. Although some real estate agencies and closing companies do offer legitimate escrow services in Mexico, your best bet is to enlist the services of a U.S. or Canadian escrow service, where it is more regulated and, therefore, more secure.

2. **Buy land that is being disputed or that is not privatized.** The most important thing to do when considering purchasing property that was once *ejidal* land is to ensure that the land has been fully privatized and that the proper notifications have been made. Do not purchase land or begin the process of purchasing land that is not fully privatized yet. Although the process can take as few as a few months, it can take as long as a few years, and the process just is not smooth enough yet to be completely reliable when it comes to solidifying a length of time. Along the same lines, do not take a seller's word if they tell you the land has been converted. It is always highly advisable to immediately check with the National Agrarian Registry to confirm the land's categorization and if it is in fact private and able to be sold. If you attempt to buy *ejidal* land without checking first with the registry, you risk losing any deposit or escrow money because the seller does not have the legal right to sell you the land and, therefore, you cannot legally buy the land.

3. **Buy into a development that is not built yet without understanding the risk.** Since initial capital is often hard to come by in Mexico, according to Matthew A. Miller, developers often use investors' money as capital toward building the development. It is important to state that there are pre-development deals that are 100-percent legitimate and offer buyers a great opportunity to purchase a unit at a discounted price. However, there are many deals — particularly for timeshares and condo units — which have risk written all over them. The potential for this kind of deal to go south is very high, as you are buying into a de-

velopment that either has not been built yet or that is not completed. Should you decide to buy into a pre-development, the key is to investigate the developer's finances, inquire about the amount of units that sold in the building, and check that he/she has obtained every necessary building permit and clearance to build on the land. Like any other deal, the bulk of your payment should go into escrow until you physically receive the title and deed to your property, and you can ensure the property is actually completed and livable. If you choose to take a deal and front, say, $100,000 for a beachfront condo, know that you are running the risk of losing your entire payment, should the development not come to fruition.

4. **Agree to let a developer handle the details of the purchase.** Linda Neil explained: "Beware of any developer who says the transfer [of title] can be done 'in house' and that the developer will hand everything to the Notary." Agreeing to this could mean problems you are not aware of until it is too late, such as problems with the title. Enlisting a good closing agent, discussed in Chapter 6, is highly advisable to avoid title problems and to oversee the entire purchasing process.

5. **Sign a contract in Spanish without understanding what it says.** Any contracts you sign should be in a language you understand. Most contracts use a dual column format, where the Spanish and English version will be included. You should never sign a contract unless you have had it translated and reviewed by an English-speaking lawyer first so you can understand every term and clause. Many people hire a bilingual attorney to advise on the legalities

of the contracts because of the language barrier. Contractual and legal terms are hard to understand, particularly when they are presented in a language you have limited familiarity with, so while it may cost more to hire an attorney to help you navigate the nuances of your contracts, it is well-worth it — and quite necessary.

6. **Make any deposit without doing a title search.** If the seller does not have the title to the property you are interested in buying, you will not be able to purchase the property. The seller must hold the legal title in order to officially transfer it to you. If you give the seller a deposit before you confirm they hold the title, you risk losing whatever money you give to them. The importance of doing the title search before any money changes hands cannot be overstated.

7. **Purchase property in the restricted zone without a bank trust.** Unless you set up a trust with a bank, you will not receive the title to your property. Legally, you will not own your property if you do not have a trust, and you will face an increased risk of extensive legal complications as well as an increased risk of ultimately losing your property.

8. **Put your property in someone else's name.** Prior to 1972 and the establishment of the bank trust, it was not uncommon for foreigners to purchase property by putting the property in a Mexican national's name, a risky move that made the buyer very vulnerable and in no legal control of their property. Even with the trust system set up today, some foreigners attempt to get around the system by setting up their title in someone else's name.

Some buyers are actually convinced to do so with promises of saving time and money, which should be the first red flag. In Mexico, people who attempt to serve as the middlemen to such illegal transactions are called "straw men." There have also been stories of straw men convincing foreign buyers to set up Mexican corporations to purchase property in the restricted zone that do not coincide with the laws regulating the process. Both transactions should be avoided, as they are not only illegal, but are likely to cause a messy and expensive legal battle in the end.

9. **Listen to anyone who tells you not to worry.** If you question your real estate agent, or any other professional you are working with during the process, and are told "not to worry," your concerns are not being addressed properly. The old way of doing things in Mexico was very unstructured and loose, which is why many buyers were roped into deals that were not in their best interest. It is why some buyers were left with no title or deed to their property while being promised everything was fine. Now, although the real estate acquisition process is more structured and investors are more protected, it is still important to be an informed consumer and to ask questions. Never take someone's word for something, particularly if you have an inkling that something is not right. If an agent or any other real estate professional you encounter suggests that you skip any step in the process in order to save time or money, you may want to consider hiring someone new. It simply is not worth it to deal with anyone who advises you to cut corners.

10. **Use a real estate agent you have not confirmed is acting in your best interest.** According to Linda Neil, unless you sign a contract that specifically states you are all right with your realtor representing both you and the seller, you should never enlist an agent who represents both parties.

11. **Believe anyone who advises you:**

    a. **That you will not have to pay capital gains tax even though you do not plan to treat your Mexican property as your primary residence.** If you plan to retire to Mexico and spend the majority of your time at your Mexican home and become a tax resident, then you will qualify for a tax break when you sell your property. If you plan to use your home as your primary residence, you will be exempt from up to $250,000 (for a single person) and $500,000 (for married couples) of the profit you make from the sale of your property. The house needs to be your primary residence for at least two years before you can benefit from the tax break. Any realtor who advises you that your property will qualify for the capital gains tax exemption when you only plan to use the property as a vacation home is ill-advising you.

    b. **That you will not need to involve a *notario publico* in your transaction.** The *notario publico* is perhaps the most important part of the Mexican real estate purchasing process. Appointed by the government, they responsible for conducting the title search and ensuring that all the documents and permits have been obtained, and the title is in order. In a nutshell, the buck stops with them. If there is any sort of legal issue with the transaction, they will uncover it.

c. **That you will not need to get a bank trust for land in the restricted zone.** If you are buying beachfront property, you will need a *fideicomiso* from a bank because foreigners are not able to directly purchase property located within 30 miles from any coastline and 60 miles from any border. The bank technically owns all property within the restricted zone and grants all rights to the land to foreigners through the *fideicomiso*. If you do not set up a trust with a bank and obtain the proper paperwork and clearance, you will not legally be recognized as a lessee of the property. Given that the bank owns all property in the restricted zone, you can easily lose your property if you do not formally create a trust and sign a contract with the bank.

d. **That a closing agent is a waste of money.** Technically, you do not need a closing agent to purchase property in Mexico. However, enlisting one can make your purchase easier, as he or she can alert you to problems and streamline the process for you.

e. **That you should set up a Mexican corporation to purchase residential property.** A Mexican corporation formed by foreign investors can only purchase property for commercial purposes, like a bed and breakfast or a restaurant. Things can get murky if you try to get around this, and it is never advised to purchase property through a Mexican corporation for residential purposes.

Bruce Greenberg of Montaña Verde Consultants, a consultancy agency that specializes in valuation and appraisals for individual buyers and developers, coined the phrase "Don't leave your brains at the border." It sounds logical enough, but it sums up the importance of taking all the cautionary steps you would take when buying property in the United States — or anywhere else in the world. You should not allow the lure of the beautiful beaches and affordable beachfront condos to mask the fact that purchasing property is a complex process that requires a full understanding of the Mexican legal system, as well as the process of purchasing real estate in a foreign country.

"Margarita Mind" is another phrase used among the locals and professionals in the industry to describe the mindset that some foreigners get into when visiting the beautiful beaches of Mexico. Too often, people will visit Mexico on vacation and see the enticing real estate options and get lured into wanting the property, and even putting down a deposit. This is more common in the larger condo and timeshare developments, where developers will lure potential buyers with enticing presentations that present low prices. Too often, the excitement and the seemingly affordable prices push investors to jump right in, either purchasing a property they cannot afford, or putting down a deposit in a development that is not complete yet.

Learning from Others' Mistakes

There have been a number of stories in the media that have highlighted the importance of being a knowledgeable investor and following each step carefully in the investment process. Investors lost millions in the Baja Beach and Tennis Club scandal, and more recently, in the Trump Ocean Club development in Baja. There have also been a number of lower-profile disputes over land in various states in Mexico, and many of them are centered on the nature and classification of land on which developments are built.

While these deals went sour and thousands of foreigners lost out on millions of dollars, time, trust, and their homes, the lessons learned from them are valuable. Future investors have the benefit of using the mistakes the investors made in these deals to prevent from making the same ones.

Since the legal framework surrounding foreign investment in Mexican real estate is fairly new, many of the disputes over land have initiated because of the non-existence of clear laws to mandate the land prior to the 1990s. Such is the case with the Baja Beach and Tennis Club.

The Baja Beach and Tennis Club

One of the most high-profile stories of an investment gone wrong was the dispute over the nature of the land on which the Baja Beach and Tennis Club in Punta Banda was built.

In the 1990s, investors plunked down millions for units in the Baja Beach and Tennis Club, located near Ensenada. Although it is unclear whether or not investors knew this at the time, the nature of the land and who held the title to the land was being disputed in Mexican court. By the time the dispute had escalated, dozens of people — many of them American and Canadian vacationers and retirees — were enjoying their homes in the luxurious development.

The issues began when the developer built on the property despite the fact that several people had come forward with titles, claiming original ownership to the land. People bought units in the development despite the fact that the title to the land was in dispute. It was initially claimed, and backed by the Federal Ministry of the Agrarian Reform, that the developer bought the property from the *ejido*. It was later discovered and determined by a Mexican court that the land was not in fact *ejidal* land, and the *ejido* who sold the developer the property was never entitled to sell it as the *ejido* never held the title to the land.

Given that the laws regulating the privatization process of *ejidal* land were not nearly as clear and developed as they are today, the land fell through the loopholes in the system. Because the developer ignored the fact that the actual owners of the land − the people who held the title to the property − had taken legal action in an attempt to recover their property, many people were literally evicted from their homes and never recovered their money.

During the course of the dispute, it was also discovered the developer ruined what should have been protected wetlands, waterways, and habitats by developing on the land. The dispute unveiled that not only did the developer build on land that was being disputed, but he also never acquired the proper building and environmental permits to develop on the land.

Unfortunately, many of the laws and regulations that exist today to protect the buyer, as well as the environment, natural habitats, and waterways of Mexico, did not exist when the legal dispute was initiated. The story of the Baja Beach and Tennis Club cast a dark shadow over the idea of foreign investment in Mexican real estate, which is quite a shame. Realistically, there are thousands of solid, legal investment deals and purchases to every Baja Beach and Tennis Club scandal. The series of events and factors that led to escalation and severity of the scandal can be easily avoided today by a number of cautionary steps.

What went wrong: The developer purchased *ejidal* land from *ejidatarios* who did not hold legal title to the land. When investors purchased units in the development, several original titleholders had already come forward to claim that the land was not owned by the *ejido* and therefore was sold under false pretenses. Investors had already given the developer millions of dollars, and it has been speculated that some knew that the title to the land was being argued over in court. In the end, investors lost their homes when the court ruled that it was not in fact *ejidal* land, and the *ejido* never had the right to sell it to the developer. Aside from the title issues, the developer also never acquired the proper building and environmental permits to develop on the property.

How to avoid a similar situation: Purchase title insurance from a legal, registered title company for the value of your property. To be entirely proactive, invest the money to do a title search on your own before you put any money down, and do not deposit any money until you have proof that the seller or developer has legal title. In the Baja Beach and Tennis Club case, the government first officially recognized the purchase by the developer, and it was only later discovered that the seller did not hold the title.

Today, investors are much more protected from situations like these, but it is still imperative to purchase title insurance, as well as to research the developer's permits to ensure he or she has proper clearance to build on the land. Hiring a consultancy agency that specializes in Mexican real estate is also a wise investment, as their job is to investigate subjects like environmental and building permit clearance.

The Trump Ocean Resort Baja

In March 2009, a story broke about the bankrupt Trump Ocean Resort in Baja, a luxury hotel and condo resort boasting more than 500 suites. Located just over a half hour from San Diego, the resort was supposed to be the first of its kind in the Baja area and was to offer investors luxury hotel amenities with the opportunity to own condo units in the towers of the development. It was a new approach to real estate, and the project was hyped as dozens of buyers plunked down millions of dollars on pre-construction, priced from a couple hundred thousand to $3 million, beginning in 2006.

In total, more than 50 different buyers put down a minimum of 30 percent each for pre-sale luxury condos in the resort, pumping more than $30 million into the development. Many were lured to make deposits on units before the resort had any development or broke any ground, during an extravagant presentation to potential U.S. buyers in southern California. They were urged to purchase on the spot to get a good deal at a pre-construction price, and many did.

The sprawling resort community was set to be partially completed in late 2008. With the crash of the U.S. stock market and the ensuing recession, the development came to a screeching halt. In 2008, after two years of development and construction, investors were informed that the project was defunct and that funds were so dried up there was no money to refund initial deposits.

With the dried up funds also came legal finger pointing. Lawyers for several investors filed a lawsuit against Trump. Although Trump, his extended family, and some of his business partners initially promoted the development, Trump claimed to have no direct involvement in the project and claimed he simply leased his name to the developer. Regardless of the technical and legal details of the story, buyers were led to believe Trump was a big part of the development, and many invested in the resort because of Trump's involvement and his reputation as a trustworthy real estate developer.

In the end, very few could have predicted the quick demise of such a promising and lucrative resort. When the project was initiated, the U.S. housing market was strong and steady, and financing and cash for capital were very easy to obtain. Many investors refinanced their primary residences in the U.S., or took out a second mortgage or line of equity on their homes to finance their Mexican purchase. When the development went belly-up, they were left with little more than their financer to answer to.

What went wrong: The developer used investors' initial deposits on the luxury condo units as capital toward the construction and development of the resort. When the U.S. housing market crashed and the country entered into a recession, the development went bankrupt and had no funds left to return investors' deposits. As a result, dozens of buyers lost millions of dollars in deposits when the project ran out of money and could not be completed.

How to avoid a similar situation: What happened with the Trump resort is an example of the kind of risk you must be aware of prior to making any deposit on a pre-construction property. Without putting your money in a U.S. FDIC-insured escrow company, there is no guarantee you will get your money back if the development does not get completed.

Purchasing any pre-construction unit is a risk to both your money and your time, but much more often than not, pre-construction purchases prove to be wise and profitable investments. The best way to protect yourself and your money and to minimize your risk is to deposit any required funds to a licensed escrow company. When you do so, you are ensuring that the developer does not use your money as capital for the project and instead receives the money when you receive the keys to your property.

The Tulum Real Estate Dispute

This dispute over the nature of land in a small beach town outside Cancun is interesting and complicated. Tulum was once a little-known town with gorgeous beaches and ancient Mayan ruins. For its location so close to a major development area, Tulum remained virtually untouched by developers and foreigners alike.

Several years ago, a number of different investors purchased property in the area and developed commercial properties, including hotels and bed and breakfasts. Since then, the area has grown and transformed from a small, unknown beach town to an attractive vacation and real estate investment spot for a higher-end crowd. In 2008, the federal government raided several hotels in Tulum and forced their abrupt shut down, claiming the properties were not legal and that the investors did not obtain proper permits to develop on the land. The hotel owners claimed the development of their hotels and succeeding renovations to the property predated any laws requiring such permits and environmental assessment requirements. Moreover, the state government issued them titles to the property without any of the said requirements.

The nature of this dispute is complicated particularly because some of the legal foundation precedes the existing laws and regulations established by the Mexican government. Since the idea of foreign investment in real estate and real estate development in general is fairly new, there are a number of disputes like this one that fall into the loopholes created during the transition and revamping of the legal system.

The interesting part is the dispute between the state and the federal government and the seeming contradiction of the two legal systems. The federal government claimed the development of the hotels on the land was a violation of environmental laws, and claimed that an environmental impact study prior to any development should have been done because the land was a protected national park. The buyers claimed they filed and received all the right paperwork when purchasing the property and received titles from the state government.

As the details of the dispute were uncovered, it was discovered that the land was in fact once a national park more than 25 years ago, but when the land was initially converted, the legal process was not done correctly. When the state government sold the land, therefore, the land was never properly declassified, and the investors who purchased the land were left with titles to the land that may not have been legally granted in the first place.

What went wrong: Investors bought land that was never properly privatized that was decreed as a national park by the federal government. The state government sold parts of the land to investors, who received legal titles from the state government. Investors were unaware that their land was never properly reclassified and cleared for sale until the federal government forced the closure of a handful of hotels in the area, claiming the investors never had the proper permits and environmental clearance to build on the land.

There is a similar legal dispute in a high-end Los Cabos town home development. More than ten years ago, the developer purchased land that was never properly privatized and ultimately built a residential condo development. As of September 2009, investors in the development were at risk because the land was never properly converted. Unfortunately, unless the issue gets resolved in court in the developer's favor, owners face the risk of losing their property.

How to avoid a similar situation: Fortunately, this is a very unique situation. The land involved in this dispute dates back to before the transition and reevaluation of several real estate and consumer protection laws and regulations, and it falls into a loophole in the system.

While it may be nearly impossible to avoid a situation similar to this, hiring a sharp attorney and even a consultant company to research the land for you is a smart strategy. Title insurance companies also conduct extensive title searches and likely would be able to identify any potential issues like the ones involved in the Tulum and Los Cabos areas. Particularly in areas where there is limited development and foreign investment, it is wise to enlist legal and other professional guidance before you buy. Of course, purchasing title insurance is also imperative to protect you against title and land disputes such as this one.

These disputes are mere representations of the variety of issues you can encounter during the process of purchasing real estate. Although the process of foreign investment in real estate is becoming easier, and consumer protection laws are certainly improving, the lesson here regardless is *caveat emptor*, or "buyer beware." Use these stories to learn what to avoid and to ensure that your investment, as well as your time and your money, is protected.

Taking the Right Steps

So what *should* you do to ensure your purchase is safe and secure? Linda Neil advises her clients and those considering purchasing property in Mexico to consider the following guidelines when acquiring real estate in Mexico. Many of these will be discussed in greater detail in later chapters.

1. Enlist a real estate agent who is listed with AMPI.

2. Ensure that your real estate agent is not also representing the buyer, which would be a conflict of interest but is not entirely uncommon in Mexico.

3. Consider staying away from *ejidal* land. Although the government continues to make foreign purchase of *ejidal* land easier, it is still a long and involved process that can take many years.

4. Make sure that the seller you are dealing with in all transactions is the legal owner of the property. If he or she is not, make sure the property is being handled and managed by the legal power of attorney. Ask for documentation for both.

5. Insist on a binding arbitration clause in your contract, which would protect you from many avoidable litigation circumstances.

6. Do a title investigation. You can either do your own — which may mean paying an additional $1,100-$1,300 — to save time in the process, or wait for the *notario publico* to check the official status of the title.

7. Get title insurance. Make sure the insurance is worth the value of your property. Title insurance will protect your property if for some reason you are unable to get the proper title from the seller for your property.

8. Consider the costs of closing and get an estimate of the costs in writing. Closing costs are significantly higher than closing costs in the U.S. and should be budgeted from the beginning.

9. Use an escrow service for your payment until you receive the deed to the property, which must be signed by all parties.

10. Make sure you receive a registered, legal title document when your property is transferred.

11. Understand the variety of taxes involved in your purchase.

12. To fully protect your investment, hire a third party to supervise the title transfer process, which will also ensure the process of escrow, title and deed transfer, and closing procedures go smoothly.

According to Chris Snell of Snell Real Estate, the following four rules apply to those purchasing property in Mexico:

"Rule No. 1: Never give your money
to a seller until you get a title.
Rule No. 2: Always get your title (trust);
Rule No. 3: Always get U.S. Title Insurance.
Rule No. 4: See rule numbers one through three.
Remember: This is a buyer-beware country,
much like many others in the world.
Rules one through three are for your
safety and protection— no one else's."

Undocumented Transactions

Many professionals in the Mexican real estate industry advise buyers that a simple due diligence, along with a little common sense, will go a long way in securing your transaction. Just as in any other country, or with any other financial or business investment, you should ensure you take every step necessary to secure your real estate purchase. This includes properly documenting your transaction, such as registering your transaction with the public registry and providing and applying for all the necessary permits and paperwork. Skipping one step or taking the wrong advice of any professional who downplays the necessity of such paperwork and permits could cost you your home.

Although your attorney, closing agent, any title company you hire, and the *notario publico* are responsible for ensuring your property is fully researched and clear of any tax, lien, or title issues, it is always best to double-check yourself. Being aware of the requirements of the Mexican legal system will greatly enable you to monitor the process and ensure your transaction is documented and secure. Should you come across anyone, including the seller, who is unwilling to provide tax, title, or any other required documents, take it as a precautionary sign that something may be wrong with the property.

CHAPTER 6

Parties Involved in the
Home Buying Process

When you purchase property in Mexico, you will deal with a number of different professionals. There are, however, a few key differences in the roles that each person plays that are crucial to understand.

In general, you will work with the following professionals and companies throughout the process of your Mexican purchase:

- A real estate agent representing the seller, and possibly a buyer's agent representing your own interests as a buyer

- A *notario publico* who will research and secure the title to your property

- A bilingual closing agent who will review legal documents and permits

- A Mexican bank, if you are buying property in the restricted zone

- An appraiser who will appraise your property for tax purposes

- A title insurance company

- The developer or seller

Depending on how you plan to purchase your property, you may involve an escrow company, a mortgage company or financer, a consultancy agency to determine any environmental or building issues, and a closing agent to oversee title transfer and the closing process.

Your first step is to choose a real estate agent to represent you, to show you properties and help determine exactly what you are looking for. Some people prefer not to enlist an agent in the beginning of their search, and often look for properties on their own and enlist an agent's help when they find something they are interested in. Either way, understanding how the system operates and what you should expect out of your agent and other professionals you encounter over the course of your purchase is essential.

The Role of the Real Estate Agent

In most Mexican states, real estate agents are not required to be licensed, and essentially anyone can serve as a real estate agent. The protection and licensing requirements that exist in the United States and other countries to ensure buyers are protected against fraudulent representatives do not exist in Mexico, but will soon. "The states of Sinaloa and Sonora now require licensing, and others are close behind," Linda Neil said.

Finding a Trustworthy Agent

Finding a realtor you like and trust is the key to beginning a successful property search. Because real estate agents in Mexico do not need a license, the industry is therefore a less regulated profession. To ensure you are working with a trustworthy and experienced agent, check that he or she is a member of the Association of Mexican Real Estate Professionals (AMPI). You can do this by visiting **www.ampi.org**.

"AMPI is a national organization, affiliated with the National Association of Realtors® (NAR) and the International Federation of Real Estate Professionals (FIABCI). AMPI members have a Code of Ethics similar to that of NAR and are entitled to call themselves realtors," explained Linda Neil. There is a distinction between those real estate agents who are members of the National Associate of Realtors® and those who are not.

Like the process in the United States, a real estate agent represents almost all Mexican properties. Mexico has online Multiple Listing Services (MLS), where you can easily navigate properties by geographical area and narrow your search by area, property type, and price. In most instances, each town or city has its own MLS. AMPI also has a multiple listing service on their Web site, **www.ampi.org**. Most local chapters of AMPI, such as AMPI Los Cabos for instance (**www.ampiloscabos.com**), also have multiple listings for that particular area.

In the Mexican real estate industry, recommendations and references go a long way. Unlike many agents in the United States, who have to hold a real estate license to sell real estate, agents in Mexico are not always held to any such standards. Therefore, word-of-mouth is valuable, and you should always ask for references before you begin any transaction with a Mexican real estate agent.

How does the role of a real estate agent in Mexican differ from the role of an agent in the United States?

Chris Snell of Snell Real Estate explained: "The legal system in the U.S. really governs and punishes agents if they deceive a buyer or seller. Here in Mexico, it is the broker who has to make the rules that the agents must abide by. We oversee every real estate transaction start to finish to make sure all funds remain in Escrow, and that the transaction is safe and secure for both parties. There is very little government intervention in the practices of a real estate agent in Mexico, and the new governing groups, i.e. AMPI, are just being established."

Top Ten Questions to Ask a Realtor

1. Are you a member of AMPI?

2. What markets do you specialize in?

3. What types of properties are you able to show me?

4. Can you provide me with a list of all your services, and what you are responsible for throughout the purchasing process?

5. Do you work for a real estate agency, or are you a free-standing agent?

6. Do you have at least three references I can contact?

7. How long have you practiced real estate?

8. Do you have any experience selling real estate to foreigners?

9. Do you represent both parties, the buyer and the seller, or do you work exclusively with either one?

10. What kind of commission do you charge?

Using these questions as a guideline to selecting a real estate broker will help ensure the agent is acting in your best interest.

Unfortunately, while there are many agents who are trustworthy and professional, there do still exist those agents who are out to take advantage of buyers. They attempt to lead buyers down risky paths of investment and can make suggestions that do not benefit the buyer. Knowing the basics of the Mexican legal system that governs foreign investment in real estate is crucial and will arm you with the basic knowledge you need to be able to determine if a real estate agent is not trustworthy or acting in your best interest. Without some common knowledge of the process, your risk of being taken advantage of is much higher.

> The general rule of thumb when choosing a real estate agent and beginning the process of purchasing is to do your due diligence. Take time to research any real estate agent you consider working with, ask for references, and most importantly, *ask questions*.

For the most part, professionals in the industry know each other and can recommend colleagues in the field. The best thing to do is to ask for a recommendation once you research and feel comfortable enough to secure your initial contact. If you plan on financing your purchase, many of the mortgage companies that specialize in cross the border financing for foreigners know lots of people in Mexico, and asking them to recommend an agent, an attorney, or a title insurance company is a great first step.

How do I know what kind of real estate agent or broker to choose? What if I want to look at all types of properties?

Snell recommends: "If you work with a leading broker in a major market, they can show you everything so you can compare one home to another. If you go and work with a developer's sales staff that only represents that development, you are only going to see what is available in that development. On the flip side, if you work with a broker that does not represent developments, then they will not be able to show you the comparables within area developments. The key is to find a broker that represents developers and handles the general real estate market as well."

The Buyer's Agent

The buyer's agent is responsible for showing you property available for purchase within your financial, geographical, and lifestyle requirements; negotiating a price and terms of contract that are within your best interest; advising on financing possibilities; preparing the initial tax and title documentation; and arranging inspections. According to an article titled "Agency and the Real Estate Agent," author Linda Neil states that the buyer's agent "should assist the client in locating the best property possible which will meet buyers' requirements. Once located, the property should be inspected as to suitability for the purpose intended and the most attractive price and terms possible negotiated for the acquisition of the property."

The Seller's Agent

"Simply put, the seller's agent has the obligation to counsel his seller as to fair and reasonable selling price, as to the importance of disclosure of defects in the property. The seller's agent should plan to offer the property to the widest audience possible. The purpose of this, if course, is to obtain the highest price possible for the property," according to Agency and the Real Estate Agent.

For the simple reason that a buyer's agent should be negotiating the lowest purchase price for you and the seller's agent should be negotiating the highest purchase price for the seller, it is never wise to enlist an agent who represents both parties. "A conflict of interest is inevitable," said Neil.

General Real Estate Practice Guidelines

To get an idea of what your agent should be doing for you and what you can expect when it comes to commission and sharing responsibilities, Neil has created the following guidelines to advise her clients, and buyers in general, on typical real estate etiquette. She advises that these are only guidelines and that they may vary from area to area. Generally speaking, however, the following should apply:

1. The buyer, under the advisement of their real estate agent and closing agent, should select the escrow company to protect funds.

2. The seller should determine the agent's sales commission prior to listing the property, which is typically a percent-

age of the purchase price (not the listing price). Commission should be secured in writing via a contract between the seller and the agent or the agent's company.

3. Commission should never be paid directly to the agent but rather to agent's company.

4. The real estate company representing the buyer and the real estate company representing the seller usually split the commission earned from the sale.

5. If a buyer is referred to an agent from a previous agent, the referral fees range from 20 to 25 percent of the real estate company's commission. This will not directly affect you, but it is good to know.

The Role of the Notario Publico

The importance of the role of a *notario publico* cannot be overstated. Unlike an American notary public, the *notario publico* plays a crucial role in the purchasing process and serves as the legal appointed by the Mexican state government. *Notario publicos* are highly regarded and must meet a variety of standards in order to practice. They must pass a stringent examination, and the governor of the state where they are practicing must appoint them.

Their role is to act on behalf of the Mexican government to oversee the purchasing process and to ensure a foreign buyer's transaction is legal. They are legally responsible for drafting the title document for your property and for ensuring that your transaction follows the legal requirements as outlined by Mexican real estate law.

The *notario publico* is responsible for:

- Reviewing the No Liens Certificate to determine that the title has no current liens and the title can be transferred

- Reviewing the Property Tax Certificate to be sure that all property taxes have been brought current by the seller

- Reviewing the official appraisal to determine taxes owed at closing

- Calculating and paying the acquisition and capital gain taxes caused by the transaction

- Drafting the deed and formalizing the signatures of the buyer and seller to legally bind the deal

- Recording the sale of the property and the transfer of title with the public registry of property

A *notario publico* costs significantly more than a notary public in the Unites States because their role is much more involved. Typically, these fees are the responsibility of the buyer and are usually 1 to 1.5 percent of the sale price of the property. Additionally, you will be required to pay a value-added tax, known in Spanish as *Impuesto al Valor Agregado* (IVA), which is 10 to 15 percent of the value of services provided. IVA taxes have to be paid to *notario publicos*, appraisers, and any other people you enlist who provide professional services.

Their responsibilities stop short of being legally responsible for an exhaustive title search.

The Role of the Closing Agent

An experienced closing agent is another key person in the real estate purchasing process. Hiring a good closing agent who understands the ins and outs of the Mexican legal system and the requirements of the law as it relates to foreign investment will make your transaction go much smoother. Developers for new construction properties almost always use a closing agent.

The closing agent may or may not be an attorney. The closing agent's company will have closing officers who know the transfer process and should have attorneys on staff if there are difficulties or glitches in the transaction. The closing agent should be involved in drawing up your promissory agreement contract (discussed in Chapter 9) and reviewing all your documents, including your title, certificate of no encumbrances, and your permits. A closing agent also order a complete title search before the deal reaches the *notario*, which will save you valuable time and money should there be a problem with the title.

> "The Settlement Company is the pioneer of the virtual closing, a process by which you can handle everything from your home or on the beach," said Neil, the company's founder.

Although having a contract with a closing agent is not always necessary, it can be helpful to outline exactly what services the closing agent will be providing.

"Professional closing agents should have bilingual attorneys and experienced closing officers on-staff to review the legalities of your transaction and to ensure that all the documents received from the *notario* are in order. Prudent buyers also enlist the help of closing agents, companies like The Settlement Company®, who can oversee the permit process, review the draft of the deed being used in the transfer of title and order the title investigation, identifying any problems before the title has been transferred and money exchanged," said Neil.

The closing agent's job is crucial. Although the notary's job is to confirm the validity of all your documents and to confirm the validity of your title, there have been instances where the notary public overlooks a thing or two, says Neil.

For example: A foreigner goes to purchase a property that was privatized from *ejidal* land 10 years ago. During the notary's review, the first right of refusal — a required step to privatization of *ejidal* land before it can be sold — is not mentioned in the prior deed, no issues come up, and the title is deemed clean and transferred to the new buyer. However, years later members or heirs of the *ejidal* group come back to reclaim the land. It is found that when the land was privatized, certain legal proceedings were not complied with, and the privatization process was incomplete. The buyer must then face a legal battle to defend the property and may indeed lose it.

Even though the *notario* is responsible for reviewing the certificates, he or she cannot be held responsible if the title has defects. This is where enlisting the services of an independent closing agent or title company to supervise the transfer can be extremely beneficial, and can save you money and time. Specialized companies like The Settlement Company provide these services and can ensure there are no complications in the process of acquiring the title.

Finding a Trustworthy Closing Agent

The requirements for attorneys are similar to those in the United States and other countries. Attorneys must be licensed, and clients should never hesitate to ask for his or her license, which will include a license number and a photo of the attorney. Reviewing the document will ensure that the person you are working with is legally allowed to practice law in Mexico. As an additional precaution, buyers should hire a lawyer who is independent of the seller, the seller's agent, or even the buyer's agent. It is best to get an unbiased, freestanding legal opinion than to have an attorney with any involvement in the deal outside of your relationship with them.

Questions to Ask a Closing Agent:

1. Do you work for a company or independently?

2. If you work for a company, do you have attorneys on staff, and do they have professional degrees?

3. What kinds of fees do you charge?

4. What exact services will you provide?

5. Do you work for a company or do you practice on your own?

6. What areas of law or real estate that you specialize in?

7. Can you help me determine taxes and closing cost expenses?

8. Will you order or conduct a title search?

9. Can you provide at least three references?

10. Do you have experience with foreigners, Mexican bank trusts, and foreign investment?

11. How long have you been in business and offering closing services?

Linda Neil also recommends asking your closing agent how he/she handles funds received for closing and if he or she prepares specific instructions to the escrow company and other parties involved for dispersing the funds.

Closing agents do not have to be specifically licensed in Mexico to be able to advise you on a real estate purchase. However, take caution just as you would when researching a real estate agent. Ask for credentials and references. The more experienced the staff and in-house counsel are in handling foreign investment transactions, the better off you will be. This does not mean, however, that someone who has limited experience in handling foreign investment transactions is not qualified. In the end, common sense and a little research go a long way.

The Role of the Appraiser

In order to transfer title to you, Mexican law requires that an appraisal of the property be done to establish the amount of taxes to be paid at the closing, particularly the transfer tax. The closing agent or the municipal government will generally select the appraiser, and the appraiser's job is to set a value for the property based on values established by the municipal government. Quite often the appraised value of a property is less than the sale value, but it is very important for the buyer to insist upon declaring the full price paid in the deed, as this establishes the tax basis for future transactions.

The appraiser appointed by the municipality is different than an independent appraiser whom you may choose to hire to establish the market value of a home (and not the value for tax purposes). Consultancy agencies like Montaña Verde (MV) can provide an independent and initial appraisal of your property, which you can use as leverage to negotiate a price. While MV usually works with higher-priced real estate, it is not a bad idea to hire an independent appraiser to advise you on the value of your property or to obtain comparable prices from your real estate agent. This is an excellent negotiating tool.

The Role of the Mexican Bank

If you are purchasing property in Mexico's restricted zone, you will be dealing with a bank to set up a real estate trust, known as a *fideicomiso*. Since the establishment of the trust system in 1972, many banks offer trust services, which are usually smooth and reliable. Many of the banks in Mexico that offer trusts to foreigners are actually international and include well-known banks like Deutsche and HSBC.

The professionals you enlist to help you in your search will have relationships with banks to set up a trust. You as the buyer can also research the fees and terms that different banks offer and decide which bank you would like to use. Often, if buyers are working with a reputable real estate agent, they will automatically approach a larger international bank that they have a relationship with to set up the trust.

Although the process and fee schedule for acquiring and setting up trusts is being streamlined so that every bank offers the same services under the same conditions according to the federal government, it still varies slightly from bank to bank.

Three Things to Consider Before You Decide on a Bank:

1. The terms and length of the trust. According to federal law, trusts are granted for a period of 50 years and can be renewed

2. The annual fee the bank charges to maintain your trust

3. Any additional fees the bank charges on top of the trust fee, which may include permit fees and power of attorney fees, among others

The Developer

If you are purchasing a single-family home as opposed to a condo or villa in a development, you will deal directly with a seller and his or her agent. In Mexico, condominium and timeshare developments are very popular among American and Canadian investors, in which case the seller may be a developer or builder.

In many ways, dealing with a developer is easier than dealing with a private owner as many developers have all their permits and titles in order and often have a sales team and a staff of other professionals, which makes the transaction go smoothly. Many developers are well-known in Mexico, and the more successful projects they have built and completed, the better off you are as a potential buyer. Word spreads quickly in the real estate industry in

Mexico, and most likely, you will hear about the more high profile developers as you get farther along in the purchasing process.

Things to Consider Before Working with a Developer

As the seller, the developer is responsible for obtaining the proper permits, enlisting a reputable real estate agent, and holding the title to the property. Developers operate a little differently in Mexico than they do in the United States, and it is in your best interest to know exactly how these differences can affect your purchase.

Developers in Mexico have a bit more leeway when it comes to financing and building requirements. Developers in Mexico, for instance, are not required to have financing secured before they can begin construction. They can also sell units in their development before financing is completely secured, which is why many sell units as pre-construction and use investors' deposits to fund construction and building.

Just like when hiring a real estate agent, you should thoroughly research a developer before considering investing in a property they have built. Some things you should research before investing with a developer:

Any other properties and communities the developer has built or been involved in. This will give you a great idea of not only how successful the developer has been in the past, but the experience the developer has. It is also an ideal way to visualize the types of amenities and quality of construction in the development, which will give you an idea of what you can expect in the development you are considering. It is important to ensure that the developer has in fact been involved in other projects, and it is not a bad idea to talk to people who have bought into completed development communities. If your developer has built other projects, consider asking your realtor or the development's sales team if you can speak to someone who has already bought a unit in a finished development. Ask the following questions:

- Was the developer easy to work with, and did he or she provide all the information and documentation you asked for?

- Did you use escrow?

- Was construction completed on time?

- Did the developer have clear title to the property before he or she began construction, and was he or she willing to show you the title and building permits?

- Did you run into any problems or issues with the developer during your purchase?

Buying from a developer who has not built many other developments in the area is not necessarily a bad idea, as long as the developer has solid financial backing and the details of your purchase are spelled out in a written contract. "Dealing with a new developer is easier because they are eager to sell," said Matthew A. Miller of ConfiCasa Mortgage International.

You will most likely get the most honest answer from someone who has gone through the same experience. It is wise to ask around, even when you are not considering a development and you just want to find out about an area.

Whether your deposit and others' will be used as capital toward the development. Developers in Mexico often used buyers' deposits as capital toward construction and building. If you encounter a developer who does this, it is not necessarily a red flag, but you need to fully understand the risk. If you invest in a property where the developer is using your money to build the development, you risk losing your deposit. Many people take the risk if the developer is well-known, as these types of deals can be opportunities to buy at a discounted price.

The developer's financial holdings. Do not be hesitant to ask the developer about capital, how he or she is financing the development, and how much money has been invested in the property. It is important to know what bank or financial institution is providing financing to the developer. Although it is not uncommon for a developer to use buyers' deposits as financing for the project, you should be wary of any developer who has no other means of financing.

In Mexico, developers and financers do not use bonds, which would be the most secure method of holding funds for the buyer, so unless the developer uses an established and regulated escrow company to hold funds until units are completed, there is no guarantee you will receive a refund on your deposit if something goes wrong. Like the situation in the Trump resort in Baja where the developer ran out of money, construction had to be halted, and investors lost their deposits, you risk losing not only your deposit, but also your property, if it is not secure.

The status of the title. As with any real estate purchase, you should never buy into a development or put money down on a condo, town home, or timeshare unit if the developer does not have the title to the property. In Mexico, developers are able to sell units without having all the capital to fund the entire development, which means units are often sold at very early stages of building. Regardless, a developer should hold title to the property before he/she sells any units.

Any investors with a stake in the project. Developers have been known to finance projects through multiple investors. It is wise to know what other people and companies have an interest in the development and how exactly they are involved. If you buy into a co-op, you are buying into the entire development as an investor, and you should know of all other parties who hold a financial interest in the development. As a shareholder, it is important to know the financial soundness of the entire co-op.

The percentage of units sold in the development. This can be a crucial determinate, as the more units the developer has sold, the more likely it is that the development will be a good investment. You do not want to buy into a development that the developer is having trouble selling to people.

Moreover, if a developer uses buyers' deposits to fund construction, it will have a direct impact on how quickly the development is built. The more people who buy, the more building can be done. If the development has been in the construction and building phase for a few years and it is still less than 50 percent sold, it may be a sign that you will have a while to wait before construction is complete. It also increases the risk that the developer will run out of financing before construction is complete.

On the other hand, if the development is nearly 100-percent sold within the first year of construction, it is a good sign the process may go more quickly. It is also a sign that you may be making a wise investment. Do not, however, take the percentage of units sold as a guarantee that you should buy in the development or make a deposit without escrow on a pre-construction unit. It is merely a sign that if the developer is using funds from buyers' deposits, then the likelihood of the project having a more finite construction completion date is greater.

Your rental options. Many development communities have restrictions on renting. Some require you live in your home for a minimum amount of time before you rent, and other developments do not allow renting at all. This is a big consideration if you plan on supplementing your investment with a rental income, so it is important to check the regulations of the development.

Environmental clearances and building permits. As with any potential investment in Mexico, ensuring that the developer has the title to the property as well as all the proper building permits is essential. If the developer does not have the proper paperwork and meet the proper requirements, you, as an investor, risk losing your property if a legal battle ensues. It is best to hire a consultant to research the history of the land and the title. If the land was once *ejidal* land, which you may or may not know at the beginning of the process, you should budget for hiring a consultant to do a thorough search of the history of the land.

When people buy into a development, they often assume the developer has all the proper clearances, but the truth is, many times they do not. Such is the case in a high-profile Los Cabos townhouse development, where the developer built and sold many units on land that was never properly privatized (as of August 2009, the case had not gone public yet, and the name had to be anonymous). You, as the buyer, will ultimately pay the price, and you risk losing your home if a legal battle over the land ensues and a Mexican court rules against the developer.

The escrow services used. Developers should use a reputable, legal escrow company to transfer funds until the development is complete and a sale is made. If a developer is not willing to use an escrow service, be wary. Many do not use escrow companies because they use investors' deposits as capital toward construction.

The terms of the contract. Especially if you are making a deposit to a developer without the use of an escrow account, make sure the terms of deposit are detailed very specifically in your contract. Will the developer refund your money if the development halts or cannot move forward? Make sure your contract includes a clause that states that your funds will be released if these terms are not met.

It is also important to ensure that the beginning and end date of the construction and building phase is detailed in the contract, particularly if you investing in a pre-construction unit. You do not want to invest in a development that has no end in sight. It is wise to stipulate a refund policy or a financial penalty on behalf of the developer if your unit is not ready when the developer says its will be. A clause detailing this will ensure that the developer is held accountable for completing his end of the deal in a timely manner agreed upon by both parties.

The amenities and other services included in your purchase. When you purchase in a development, you are not only buying a unit, you are buying into all the amenities the development has, from the pool and golf courses, down to the landscaping and waste disposal services. Especially if you are considering re-selling your property at some point, it is extremely important to understand exactly what amenities you will be able to use and when the amenities will be accessible.

For instance if you purchase a pre-construction unit that the developer tells you will be completed in six months, how do you know when the rest of the development will be complete? Will the pool down the block from you be open and finished by then also, or will it take longer to complete? Will landscaping, gardening, waste disposal, and other common services included in the development be available when you close on your unit?

Knowing a specific timeline for the completion of the entire development and all its amenities and services is important. If the developer cannot tell you exactly when the services and amenities will be ready, consider that the developer may not have enough capital to complete the project in a said time.

CHAPTER 7

What to Look For
in an Investment

Mexico has something for every buyer. Whether it is a $2 million beachfront villa or a $50,000 condo in a little-known fishing village on the coast, Mexico offers a wide range of investment opportunity.

With so many options, how do you go about narrowing it down? As with any real estate purchase, location is key when it comes to long-term profitability. In the end, it is important to choose a property that not only you can afford, but that you can count on to be profitable for you in the future. Even if you are not planning on flipping the property and are investing in a vacation or retirement home that you plan to own for a long time, you still want to make sure the property is a wise financial investment.

In light of the housing market crash and succeeding economic recession that began in the U.S. in 2008 and spread throughout the world, investors should expect to see drastically reduced home prices in many areas of Mexico. While this is not a terribly good thing for builders, real estate agents, and other industry-related professionals, it presents you, as a buyer, with some ideal opportunities to purchase affordable real estate in areas that will ultimately bounce back.

Areas where condo prices are high and comparable to U.S. prices often struggle most during a recession because the excessive development of the area requires a steady stream of buyers. In times of slow growth, high traffic and popular areas that depend on an influx of high-end buyers to sustain development can offer the opportunity to purchase property for a fraction of the price.

Buyers should take caution, however, when buying in an overdeveloped and overbuilt area that has seen limited growth in the past year or two, as it could be a sign the area has depreciated in value overall. You should never invest with the hopes that your property will increase dramatically in value in the future. Although many investors have realized excellent and steep profits from their Mexican investment, it should never be your No. 1 priority.

With an exception to hit the housing market took in 2008-2009, the Mexican real estate market remains strong and steady, but counting on a high profit from your purchase to supplement any financial strains the purchase will put you in is never a good idea. In other words, if you cannot afford to buy something now, do not buy it. Many people count on the profit of their property's sale in the future to ultimately reimburse them for any money they invest in the property. However, this is only healthy if you can afford to invest in the first place, and the purchase will not put you under any financial strains. That being said, one of the biggest draws to the Mexican real estate market is its affordable property and its potential for profit, and if you are able to finance it without undertaking any hardships, your purchase can be one of the best investments you will ever make.

> The key to taking advantage of today's real estate market is to tread carefully and to invest in areas that are likely to regain their popularity, and in homes that will ultimately regain their value.

Five Signs of a Good Real Estate Market

1. **Home prices in the area you are considering buying have retained their value for the most part through the global recession of 2008-2009.** Almost every home in the United States depreciated in value when the real estate market collapsed. Mexican markets were hit even harder because most Americans and other foreigners had little capital and financing to purchase vacation and second homes. Home prices in Mexico depreciated as well, but it is a good sign if the prices have retained the majority of their value prior to the market crash of 2008.

2. **Home prices and types of property vary on a small scale.** You want to look at areas that offer a range of investment options and not just one type of property in one price range. The variation of home prices and types will draw and interest a diverse group of buyers. On the other hand, areas that vary dramatically in home prices may show signs of an unsteady market that has not drawn enough people to define it yet.

3. **American stores like Walmart and Costco Wholesale are in the area.** Unless you are looking for a more authentic Mexican town or city, investing in areas that have lots of growth and large stores and shopping centers is usually a great idea. It is a sign that the area probably has a large foreign — particularly American — community of expatriates, retirees, and vacationers. These areas often have the more expensive real estate, but also have the most development.

4. **New condo, timeshare, and retirement developments are going up.** This sign may be a little tricky, as you do not want to confuse new growth with overdevelopment. Areas like Baja North that were initially hot spots for buyers from Arizona and California are now overbuilt, and developers are having problems selling units. These areas may never fully regain their popularity among foreigners, and ultimately the real estate in these areas may not either. Areas like Puerto Vallarta, on the other hand, are seeing new growth despite the hit the market took in 2009 from the recession. If you are seeing empty developments, foreclosure signs all around town, and developers almost desperate to sell you a unit, it may be a sign that the area is overbuilt and real estate may not regain its initial value.

5. **You hear buzz about the area.** When you begin to look for properties, you will be able to tell pretty quickly which areas are the hot spots among foreigners. Once you discuss what you are looking for with your broker, he or she will tell you what areas are popular for second home, vacation home, and retirement home buyers. You should also ask around. Asking a combination of people in the business and people who

have actually bought homes in Mexico will offer the most accurate idea of which up-and-coming areas to consider.

There are a variety of ways to maximize your Mexican property investment so that you can reap the financial rewards of property ownership and even generate an income from your investment. Renting out your property is an ideal way to generate cash flow from your investment, but even if you do not plan to rent, there are a variety of factors that can help secure a profit.

Renting Options

Renting your home out is the ideal way to generate an income from your purchase. Many foreigners who purchase property in Mexico as a second or vacation home rent out their property for part of the year. Especially if you are considering spending only a fraction of the year at your home, renting for the months you are not there may be a viable option.

What to Consider When Renting

With renting come additional expenses and responsibilities, including declaring and paying taxes on your rental income. "Income earned on rental income, whether a small amount or a great deal, is subject to Mexican tax," Linda Neil said. "Tax declarations must be filed monthly and failure to do so can result in heavy penalties. It is a complex process for foreigners. Many management companies do not know how to make the proper filing." Neil's company, The Settlement Company, is one of the only companies in the country to offer rental income tax filing services to foreigners.

You as the owner of the property are ultimately responsible for ensuring your property is secure, protected, and maintained. The role of landlord can require a lot of attention and work, especially if you plan to do the work yourself and not hire a property manager to act in your place when you are not there.

If you are considering renting your property, there are many Web sites and real estate companies that list rentals in your area. Web sites including **www.beachhouse.com**, **www.mexicanvacation-rentalhomes.com**, and Vacation Rentals by Owner, **www.VRBO.com**, are good sites if you want to rent your home for a short period of time. If you are looking to rent for more than a few weeks of the year, contacting a real estate company in your area is a good idea, as they will be able to identify potential long-term renters.

Things to Consider Before You Decide to Rent Your Property

1. **How many months of the year will I be spending at my home?** If you are going to be spending more than six months a year in your Mexican home, it may not be worth it to find long-term renters. You may want to consider renting for a week or two at a time to vacationers, instead.

2. **Does my home need a lot of repairs or any extensive renovations?** If any major renovations or repairs are needed to make your property livable and safe, you should make them before you rent it out. Not only will the repairs make the property more attractive to renters, but also it will secure the property's value. Problems left untreated can lead to more serious and expensive renovations down the line.

3. **Can I afford a property manager?** Hiring a property manager is a must if you will not be available in person on

a regular basis. Property managers can cost a significant amount but are often well-worth the price.

4. **Am I comfortable with renters in my home?** Ultimately, this is a big factor if you are going to treat your home as a vacation or second home for you and you family. Are you comfortable with strangers living in your house? Some people are not and prefer not to rent their property.

Hiring a Property Manager

It is a challenging task to serve as a landlord to rental tenants when you are thousands of miles away back home in your primary residence. If you plan to be out of the country where you are renting your home for an extended period time, it is advisable to hire a property manager to oversee the property in your absence.

With the increasing popularity of investors renting properties, the demand for high quality and trustworthy property management services has also increased. After all, if you invest valuable time and money into a beachfront condo in Puerto Vallarta, you want to ensure that when you rent the property out, the value of the property will not depreciate, and it will be maintained in your absence.

According to "Protecting Your Home — Selecting the Property Manager," author Linda Neil stated: "Since many investors in Mexican properties live in the United States and Canada, selection of a professional management company is a must to protect the investment and obtain the highest return on the investment."

Property management companies are popular in Mexico, and offer homeowners a safe and reliable avenue to rental and property management. You, as the owner, will want to find a property manager, either through a management company or on your own, who will tend to the specific needs of your property. According "Protecting Your Home — Selecting the Proper Manager," Neil states that the following qualities determine a good property manager.

- **Reliability and experience.** Research the property manager and ask for references. If a property management company represents them, research the company, as well. They should be able to provide a list of references from previous or existing homeowners who have used their services. Neil also recommends asking a property manager if he or she is experienced in handling real properties and capable of doing physical maintenance and repairs. A property manager who does not know how to fix a leaky sink or a broken toilet is of little use to you, and hiring an inexperienced manager will only prove to be a headache for you if you have renters.

- **Honesty.** It is crucial to hire a manager who will communicate things to you. You will need to be able to rely on the manager to report issues to you, and to be honest with you if something goes wrong in your absence.

- **Diligence.** You may need to hire a property manager to maintain your property, even if you do not have renters. More importantly, if you are hiring a manager to help you secure renters, it is imperative that they be dedicated to promoting your property and are available to real estate agents and anyone else interested in showing or seeing the property. If you expect this out of your property manager, make it very clear from the beginning. Many property managers have experience in promoting properties and securing renters.

- **Accounting experience.** If your property manager is going to be managing renters and responsible for collecting rent every month, hiring someone with accounting experience or at least experience in handling money is a wise idea. Neil advises asking the following when considering a property manager:

  ➤ "Do they have a system in place that provides for honest and accurate income and outgo?"

  ➤ "Do they handle Mexican taxes and provide you with the receipts you require for your U.S. and Canadian returns?"

- **Responsibility.** This one may seem a little obvious, but it should not be overlooked. Neil said property managers should be "responsible to make sound decisions and recommendations regarding maintenance to the property." You want to hire a manager who is not only experienced and qualified but whom you trust enough to make decisions on your behalf.

In addition to all these qualities, a property management company should have a legally binding written contract for renters that you and your lawyer should review thoroughly. According to Neil, the contract should protect you as the owner of the property if any renter defaults on payment, makes unreasonable demands, or damages your property. A good contract will protect your interests.

What to Look For in Different Types of Property

In today's real estate market, there are options to buy a variety of different properties, to build a home, or to rent before buying. It is helpful to do your homework and research the pros and cons of each property type to narrow down what you can afford and what you want in a property. Finding the perfect property, after all, is a balance between solidifying what you can afford, identifying your priorities in a home, and narrowing down your options. It takes time and research, particularly if you are not in Mexico full-time and are researching from your home country.

It is recommended to rent for at least four to six months before buying. Renting will provide you the experience of living in a foreign country and help you decide on a location and a budget.

Many experts and people who have purchased homes in Mexico will tell you that before investing in a property, it is wise to rent first for a few months to get a feel for the country and the culture where you are considering spending a significant amount if time. Rental properties — depending on what kind of property and where you choose to rent — are very affordable in Mexico. The renting option is a great choice if you are not entirely ready to make the purchasing move just yet, or if you are unsure what geographical area of the country you want to buy in.

Good Investment Strategies For
Purchasing Property in Mexico

1. **Think location, location, location.** Location is everything in real estate, so by choosing a property in a popular location, there is a higher chance of appreciation when you sell.

2. **Purchase a lower-priced home in a better area.** This speaks to the importance of location. It is often wise to purchase a lower-priced, smaller property in a thriving or up-and-coming area than to purchase a higher-priced home in an all right area. The chances of your property appreciating in value are greater if your property is in a great neighborhood than if it is a nicer, bigger home in a less attractive neighborhood.

3. **Follow FONATUR.** The Mexican government is going full steam ahead with new development plans to increase tourism and foreign real estate investment across the country. Through FONATUR, the government's tourism and development agency, the government has big plans to drive traffic and tourism to Mexico by developing geographical areas and putting in attractive amenities. It is easy to find out what FONATUR's development plans are by visiting **www.fonatur.gob.mx**.

4. **Check out the neighborhood and what types of services and businesses are in the area.** Safety is often a concern among non-Mexicans who are considering purchasing property in Mexico. Just like other countries, Mexico does have its pockets of crime. Most of the popular foreign cities and beach towns like Los Cabos, Puerto Vallarta, and

Cancun are safe because the neighborhoods are well-developed and very populated. If stores like Costco and Walmart are in the area, you can be pretty sure the area is highly populated by Americans and Canadians. Reasonable access to medical facilities and airports is an important factor in making a home a good investment, as well.

Once you solidify where you want to buy and make the decision to begin the process, there are several factors to consider when it comes to types of properties. Depending on where the property you buy is, your investment options will vary, and the considerations that define a good, solid investment will change. But what should you look for in a single-family home, a condo in a development, a timeshare, or unimproved land to optimize your investment?

Single-Family Homes

Single-family homes offer a number of pros. They are more private and offer more opportunity to "make it your own." If you buy a single-family home, you do not have to be concerned with sharing common property, neighbors, and other co-op ownership issues. The cons, of course, are the non-existence of services like waste disposal and landscaping, and amenities like pools, golf courses, and maintenance services.

As with any property, location is a key factor when considering a single-family home. Look for properties that are in the lower price range of higher-priced neighborhoods but may need some work. Labor is inexpensive in Mexico (the daily average cost for a laborer is around $5), and hiring a talented team of workers to do minimal to moderate renovations will likely add more value to the house than the cost of the renovations. This is, of course, subject to the types of renovations you do and the property's location. The single-family home buyer is more of a specialized buyer than a condo or timeshare buyer, only because in Mexico, condo and timeshare properties are more popular.

Timeshares

Timeshares are very popular in Mexico because of the high population of foreigners who vacation in Mexico each year. Timeshares offer a great opportunity to spend a couple of weeks a year in a popular area of Mexico and enjoy luxurious amenities without the complications of owning property. Many timeshare companies also allow you to swap for a year to visit other timeshare properties in different countries.

In Mexico, the federal government dictates standards that timeshares and contracts should adhere to in order to protect you, the consumer. The Consumer Protection Board also has regulations that provide minimal protection for timeshare buyers. The board aims to prevent buyers from signing contracts that do not correspond with the guidelines set forth by the government to protect those who do and wish to cancel their contract by giving buyers five days to rescind their offer.

According to the article, "Is Timeshare an Investment Property?" by Jason Tremblay, timeshares can be a great investment. "Timeshare locks in the cost of your vacation accommodations for as long as you own your timeshare, whether that is years, decades, or a lifetime," Tremblay said. Although the purchase of a timeshare will not yield as high as a profit as a home or condo purchase — and may not in fact yield any profit — the value lays in the quality you get out of it. If you vacation a lot and truly love Mexico but cannot afford to purchase your own home, or do not want the responsibility of home ownership in a foreign country, timeshares are a practical option. All-inclusive timeshares can make the deal even better.

In Mexico, some of the most popular timeshares include The Grand Mayan Nuevo Vallarta and the Mayan Palace Nuevo Vallarta, just outside Puerto Vallarta.

The Best Deals for Vacation Timeshares

Marketers are often aggressive about getting buyers to invest in a timeshare because timeshare brokers often work on a commission-only basis, and competition between brokers and timeshare developers can be fierce. Because timeshares sell for much less than a house or condo, timeshare brokers have to work harder and make many more sales to make money, which is why many of them are eager to sell to you. It is wise to take caution when any person approaches you to purchase a timeshare. Many will lure potential buyers in with seemingly "too good to be true" deals, extravagant presentations and gifts, and promises of high returns on investments and benefits if the buyer purchases the timeshare before they walk out of the room. Investing in this type of stressed and hyped environment is usually risky, and there have been many stories of investors purchasing on the spot — only to regret it later.

What to Look for in a Timeshare Deal

1. **A clear written contract.** Many timeshare horror stories begin with a pushy sales promoter who encourages po-

tential buyers to sign a purchase contract and make a deposit on a timeshare property during a sales pitch. A timeshare purchase contract should be managed no differently than any other purchasing contract and you, as the buyer, should take ample time to review all the clauses and fine print with your lawyer before you sign.

As with any property purchase in Mexico, the contract should be written in Spanish and in English so you know what commitments you are making. If you are purchasing a pre-sale unit, make sure that a specific timeline is included in the contract that details when the unit will be complete, as well as the terms if the unit is not complete by the agreed-upon date.

2. **The ability to transfer points.** Corporations that sell timeshare properties will often allow you to swap properties and transfer earned points to rent a timeshare in another participating location. Details of using transfer points and restrictions should be clearly spelled out in the purchase contract you sign.

3. **What works for *you*.** There are many different timeshare options. You can buy a timeshare that allows you one or two fixed weeks a year, or floating weeks, which allow you to change your weeks. You can also buy a fractional ownership timeshare, or one that just gives you property usage rights. With so many options, you should never be convinced to purchase something that you are not comfortable with or that does not fit into your budget.

4. **A resale.** Timeshares can be extravagant and expensive, and because builders continue to develop new communities that are even bigger and more luxurious than the previous one, the prices can be high. A timeshare resale, in which you purchase a timeshare directly from an owner instead of a developer, can offer a great value and can be considerably cheaper than buying a new unit.

As with any other purchase, taking the time to research your options and decide what you can afford is the best strategy. Timeshares are a dime a dozen in some areas of Mexico, so you, as the consumer, are in the driver's seat when it comes to purchasing. Do not let any sales representative push you into signing a contract on the spot. *Always* ask to take 24 to 48 hours to review a contract and take it to your lawyer, who can advise you on the legality of the contract.

> If a timeshare sales company or anyone representing the timeshare will not allow you to take time to review the contract with your lawyer, do not sign it. Under Mexican consumer protection law, if you do sign a contract that you later decide you want out of, you have five days to cancel. Beyond that, the government does not provide any consumer protection if you decide to cancel your purchase.

There are a variety of Web sites that list timeshare properties throughout Mexico, including **www.timeshare-resale-rental.com**, and **www.sellmytimesharenow.com**, which lists timeshare properties for sale directly from sellers and do not involve a real estate agent or sales group. Resort Condominiums International (RCI) at **www.rci.com** is a corporation that sells timeshares around the world. According to RCI, the average timeshare property costs around $15,000, in addition to an annual maintenance fee.

Condominiums

Because of the luxurious five-star amenities that so many condo developments offer, vacationers and retirees alike find condo living easy and affordable in Mexico. Unlike a single-family home, condos provide the opportunity to enjoy a property without the responsibility of maintaining it.

Mexico's condominium law regulates condo ownership and defines the co-ownership of common interest property. According to the condominium law, condos are defined as any building that contains private residency units as well as common areas. Technically, when you buy a condo, you buy a specific property unit but become a co-owner of the common areas.

What to Look for in a Condo Investment

> **The establishment of the Condo Regime.** According to the article "The Legal Aspects of Living in a Condominium" by Linda Neil, the Condo Regime is a legal document that describes the development, and it must be established before the property can be registered with the Public Registry of Property. The regime includes details of the entire development, including lot sizes or unit sizes, land measurements, the boundaries of private property for individual sale, and the areas that are to be used for common purposes and available to all owners, as well as the laws governing the development that all owners will be required to adhere to.

➢ **A clear, written contract accompanied by the developments rules and regulations.** It seems logical, but the value of a detailed contract that clearly spells out the details of your purchase is essential. You should retain a lawyer who is familiar with Mexican condominium law to review your contract and advise you of any missing or unclear clauses. Among other details, the contract and rules and regulations of the development should detail:

- The escrow services used, if the developer is using an escrow company. If you do not plan to use escrow, be aware of the risk you take in making a deposit on the unit.

- Maintenance fees that state what exactly the money is going to.

- The responsibilities of the homeowners' association and the condo rules and regulations. The condo regime details of the homeowners' association's duties and responsibilities.

- Whether you have common ownership or common rights to common property. According to the article "The Legal Aspects of Living in a Condominium" by Linda Neil, "In a common interest development, [maintenance provisions] may be either commonly owned property or common rights that may be enforced as restrictions against separately owned property." In Mexico, common ownership is more common in condo developments, but it should be stated

➢ **The title.** Ensure that the developer holds the title to the property he or she is selling you and that the builder has been cleared by all environmental and building permits to specifically build a condo development on the land. If he or she does not have title or is selling units when still in the process of acquiring the title, you take the risk of losing your property down the road if the title falls through or a problem with the nature of the land is uncovered. Take what happened at the Baja Beach and Tennis Club as a prime example of the importance of ensuring that a developer holds title to the property and that the land is not being disputed before you buy.

➢ **The ability to lease or rent your unit.** You may plan on relying on a rental income to supplement your investment. Some condo developments have restrictions on rentals and leasing, so always check with the homeowner's guidelines on their rules before assuming you will be able to rent out your condo. You should also research what other condos in your unit are renting for and calculate your profit after paying maintenance fees, bills, and a mortgage — if you are mortgaging your property.

➢ **The aesthetics and function of the entire complex.** When you buy a condo, you are not just buying your unit; you are buying an investment in the entire complex. Therefore, you should ensure that the development as a whole is well-maintained.

Even though you may be considering keeping your condo for a long time, and perhaps retiring there, you should always keep the possibility of selling down the road as an option when you consider the investment. When you are considering a condo purchase, check out the entire development and think to yourself: "If I have to sell this in 10 years, how attractive will it be to a new buyer?"

According to the article, "The Legal Aspects of Living in a Condominium" by Linda Neil, the value of the development — and your individual condo unit — is preserved through the maintenance of the common areas and the development as a whole. If you notice when you tour a development that the areas do not look well-maintained, chances that the long-term value of the property will not be as well-preserved as a development that devotes time and money to upkeep of the entire community.

According to the same article, Neil stated: "More and more, absentee owners are selecting professional management companies to perform all administration and maintenance services rather than having these services performed by the homeowners' association or its board of directors." Enlisting property management services is a great idea if you are not going to be able to manage the day-to-day details of condo ownership. However, from an investment standpoint, it is wise to take an initial review of these details yourself before you purchase. It is important to have a good idea of these details before you hand off the responsibility of managing them to a property manager.

Pre-Construction and Off-Plan Investments

A pre-construction sale is the sale of a unit in a development community before the unit has been built and construction has begun. This type of sale is also referred to as an "off-plan" sale. Pre-construction sales are common in Mexico, and you can often find a good deal by buying a condo unit before the developer begins construction. However, you should be aware of the risk involved in making a deposit on a property that is not complete yet.

These are many of the things you should look for in a condo investment including: a clear written contract, an established escrow service, a developer with a strong financial backing, and the confirmation that the developer holds the title and has all the proper building permits. However, potential buyers should also do the following when considering purchasing a pre-construction property:

➢ Be sure you have a contract that details the timeline of the construction and provides a specific date that your unit will be move-in ready, as well as the date that common areas — pools, gyms, golf courses — as well as services will be up and running.

The contract should also include a clause that states that your deposit will be reimbursed should the developer miss that deadline or should the entire development fall through or go bankrupt. You can only protect yourself against losing your deposit if you use an escrow service.

➢ Research the financials of the developer and determine how the project is being funded. Becoming familiar with how the development is being financed will give you the most accurate idea of the project's stability. Many developments are extensively marketed, but few buyers take the time to determine the financials of the development; they are eager to purchase the property because it is so beautiful and enticing. Buyers often have "margarita mind" —

caught up in their adoration of Mexican land — and forget about the research that accompanies a real estate purchase. If a developer is using funds from buyers' deposits and does not have other investors or bank financing, you may want to think twice about purchasing in the development. The use of deposit funds as the main source of financing is directly dependent on how many people buy into the development. If not enough people buy properties, the development could run out of funds and cease construction.

➤ Negotiate what works for you. If you are giving a developer a deposit, especially without using an escrow company, you are taking on a big risk. In exchange for your risk, you should negotiate everything you can that works in your favor, including the best unit in terms of location within the development, customized fixtures and upgraded appliances and amenities, and — most importantly — a discounted sale price.

➤ Confirm if the development will still be under construction after you move in. Ask if the developers plan to continue renovating while you are living there and how long they will be doing construction. You want to know before buying a property if you can expect to be disrupted with construction and noise after you move in.

If you are considering a pre-construction sale, you have much to negotiate with. You have a lot of leeway to craft a more customized property with a pre-construction unit because you are essentially taking a chance with the developer and buying a property you cannot see yet. That considerate risk should be an incentive for you and the developer to make a deal that is mutually beneficial.

CHAPTER 8

Building versus Buying

In the past few years, building a home has become more appealing to foreign investors as they realize the relative ease and affordability of constructing a customized home from the ground up. The process of building — like the process of buying an existing home — has become easier in Mexico over the past few years, and the government has made a push to regulate the process.

In an effort to encourage new development, economic growth, and tourism, the government and developers alike are making it easier for foreigners to purchase plots of land and build homes. In the past, building a home — much like investing in one — was a big risk. It was difficult to find trustworthy builders and workers, and little protection for buyers existed. Today, minimal consumer protection laws — coupled with skilled developers, architectural firms, consultants, inspectors, and builders — make the process of building a home a safe and enjoyable experience.

Although many plots of undeveloped land have increased in price along with the increase in demand for land to build homes on, it is still very possible to find a great deal on an empty lot in dozens of Mexican cities and beach towns. Because Mexico's housing market is still in its early growth stage, and many beautiful and ideal locations have not yet been cultivated by developers, the chances of discovering a plot of land in a perfect location and negotiating an inexpensive sale price remains in your favor. Depending on where you purchase land, prices vary drastically and can range from $30 a square foot to more than $150 a square foot. It all depends on your location.

CASE STUDY: BUILDING A DREAM HOME

Carol Wheeler always loved Mexico. Beginning in the 1970s, Wheeler and her mother traveled from their home in Florida to Mexico each year to visit their home in Guadalajara.

"I love the values that revolve around faith, family, and friendship," said Wheeler, "and the language and the culture."

In 1989, Wheeler decided to purchase her own property in Mexico and began the search. She initially looked to purchase an existing home and did not consider building at that point, but explained: "We were shopping for an existing house, but when the opportunity [to build] presented itself, we chose building to have what we really wanted."

And what she wanted was what she got. She describes her home as "modern Mexican, with white walls, white marble floors, and angular geometry." The home has an open floor plan with skylights, a master bedroom with a private suite, two additional bedrooms for her children, a small library, a big family room, and a laundry room with a pantry. Outside, Wheeler — inspired by architect Luis Barragán — created a tropical landscape that serves as a counterpoint to the stark building, she said.

"[My house is] sort of a gallery for the beautiful things we've gathered along the way," she explained.

Wheeler's home is located in a gated community in Zapopan on the outskirts of the city of Guadalajara. Zapopan and Guadalajara offer lots to see and do and

CASE STUDY: BUILDING A DREAM HOME

boast excellent restaurants, shopping, access to medical care, and all the other amenities of a big city. Outside the center of the city, Santiago River canyon and the Primavera Forest offer a break from city life with opportunities to hike, bike, swim, and relax.

The building took about 10 months.

"[It was] an exciting experience filled with anticipation and creative energy," Wheeler said. "We were very lucky to have met a reliable contractor while house shopping. Fortunately, I can read floor plans and worked with the builder to customize the plan he proposed. He had an undeveloped lot available on a park."

It also helped that Wheeler spoke fluent Spanish, so she could communicate with everyone working on the house. The experience went by smoothly, with only minor bumps in the road that were easily fixed.

What Wheeler loves most about her home and living in Mexico is the relaxing way of life, and the friendly and caring people. "Having theater, symphony, museums, art galleries, and wonderful restaurants at hand with the beach as close as three hours by car are what I love, also," she said. In the 20 years that she has lived in her home, she has seen the real estate market change dramatically as development has driven up the value of the area's real estate.

"A [recent] newspaper article described the Bugambilias community, and in over 10 years, property values have doubled. In the years since we built for about $60,000, Walmart, Costco, Sam's Club and the beautiful Plaza Galerias shopping center were built not far from us. A much smaller house across the street from us sold for $100,000 in 2001," Wheeler explained. If she ever decides to sell her humble abode, she is virtually guaranteed at least double what it cost her to build in 1989.

Wheeler's advice for those considering building is to "choose an architect and builder carefully, and check their references. Be present on the building site to check on the work as often as possible. Get everything in writing, and have a reputable lawyer go over your contract before signing," she advised.

Currently, Wheeler works as an editor, writer, translator, and book designer for **www.mexconnect.com**. She said of her experience with building a home in Mexico: "I would do it again in a heartbeat."

The Steps to Building a Home

Like any real estate investment, building a home requires the same time, research, and strategic planning; the process of building in Mexico is very similar to building anywhere else and can take anywhere from a few months to a few years, depending on the construction team you choose; the architectural firm you hire to map out your plans; the capability and experience of the construction manager or contractor you hire to run the project; the complexity of your home design; and the location of your land.

Building a home "takes some goal-setting and a small element of risk; however, it is every exciting, and your life will be so enriched," said Suzanne Simmons, who built an eco-friendly, three-bedroom, three-bathroom home in Riviera Nayarit.

Building a home is a considerable undertaking, so you should be willing and able to dedicate a large block of time to it. Although each building procedure may vary slightly, the general process of building a home will follow these steps:

1. Choose a plot of land in an existing subdivision development. Much like the Simmons' experience that is detailed in the case study in this chapter, buying a plot of land that is within an established development enables a quicker and easier process. In their case, the developer already had title insurance on their property, and they found it easy to set up a trust with the bank and close the deal. They also used their developer as a resource to build their home, and he even served as the builder and recommended architects and workers.

Buying a plot of land in an existing development will also make running your home easier, as the development will have plumbing, electricity, sewage systems, and a water source already established.

2. Confirm the water source and the electricity and sewage systems. In Mexico, much of the land — whether built on or empty — is located within a city or town subdivision, which makes access to water, electricity, and sewage systems convenient. But if you buy a piece of land that is not within a city or town subdivision, you will be responsible for creating your own water source, as well as securing your own sewage and electrical system. For some people, this is appealing, as they are looking for a remote area to build a self-sustaining home that is not part of a development.

If you are buying in a development, you should still research the water source. The developer may have established a system within the development, or the development may use water from an outside source. If this is the case, the cost of water may be higher, and the terms may vary, so it is always best to research this thoroughly. Also, double-check the establishment of electrical, sewage, plumbing systems, and the terms of use for anything you use from the development.

3. Hire a consultant and an architect. Hiring a consultant to provide an initial survey of a piece of land you are considering purchasing is often very beneficial. Especially in more rural areas where the nature and status of the land may be unclear, a consultant is a wise investment. Companies like Montaña Verde (MV) offer consultancy, appraisal, and valuation services that can be extremely valuable when you are considering buying property. They can give you an appraised value of your land, which enables you to approach the seller with an accurate value of the property to potentially negotiate a lower sale price if the appraised value of the land is less than what the seller is asking. A consultant can also research the land and determine the existence of any environmental or building issues before you even make an offer on the property.

Though MV usually works with high-end real estate on an individual basis or advises developers and larger companies, there are other consultants who work with more moderately priced properties. Hiring an appraiser — not to be confused with a bank appraiser who determines the value of a property for tax purposes during closing procedures — can, if nothing else, give you the opportunity to pinpoint the value of your property and take that appraised value to the negotiating table.

An architect is a key part of the building process as well. They design your blueprints according to your building plans and ensure the plans are architecturally sound and meet design and engineering needs. The architect can also advise on the layout of your house and should provide guidance on how to structure your home.

Hire an architect who is familiar with your particular geographical area and the building requirements. Better yet: Hire an architect who lives or does business in the area you are building. Working with an architect who is familiar with the area from both a personal and professional standpoint is beneficial because he or she will know the area well and be familiar with the best workers, contractors, and other professionals, as well as the local building codes and requirements.

After you have purchased your land, hiring an architect to develop your plans is the next step. Some people use architects for only the planning stage and to create blueprints, but architects can provide building and construction and see the project through to the end. If you use an architect who will also build your home, be sure to confirm that the price will include everything you expect; you should have this detailed in your contract. If a firm quotes you one price and the price ends up being significantly higher when you accept their bid and officially hire them, consider rescinding your acceptance. You want to find a firm that will detail the total cost in their quote and come within 5-10 percent of that cost at the end of the process.

These are some things you should confirm with an architect before you hire him or her:

A guaranteed price. Ask the architect to guarantee the price you were initially quoted if you hire him or her. You can expect to meet some additional costs along the way, but the big costs, including labor and materials, should be agreed upon before you begin construction. A guaranteed price will protect you from paying significantly more than you initially budgeted for. Of course, if your plans change significantly — like if you decide to redesign your house and add more rooms — more labor and materials will be required, and you can expect to pay a higher price.

References. References are the best way to check the professionalism and work quality of anyone you hire, especially in Mexico. Word-of-mouth references go a long way in Mexican culture, where things are a little more laid-back and less structured. If you meet a contractor who proves to be trustworthy, ask him or her for recommendations for workers instead of choosing them yourself. The Simmons, who are profiled in the case study in this chapter, bought an empty lot within a development and used their developer to hire a team of builders and workers. Because they knew and trusted their developer, they even hired him as their builder, and he then hired his own workers. No matter whom you hire or think of hiring, ask for at least two or three references and, most importantly, check them. Nothing is more valuable than a positive recommendation and confirmation from someone who has worked with the architect. It is also a great idea to research other buildings and houses the architect has designed.

A payment schedule. If you are using an architectural firm for the entire building process, it is important to determine a payment schedule. Usually, an architect will allow you pay in stages, which ensures that everyone is paid for work as the work is done, and you approve the work in stages. Make sure a specific installment plan is included in your contract.

A construction timeline. Each stage of the building should be detailed with the specific details that will be done in each stage. A completion date for each stage should be specified as well.

4. Check city ordinances. Every city and town has its own set of building and zoning codes, required permits, and regulations. Do not purchase land and make plans to build without first checking the ordinances of the particular city where your land is located. Some city ordinances restrict the amount of property you are able to build on, and regulate other things like wall heights and location of fences. Beginning construction on a home that the city has not cleared is highly inadvisable, and it can only set you back valuable time and money if you run into a problem after you begin building.

5. Research a contractor and hire a construction manager. If you are not using an architect to also build your home, you will need to hire a reputable builder. Go about doing this the same way you would an architect: Research and ask for references. Ask for locations of buildings, houses, and developments the builder has constructed and carefully check them out. Doing so will give you a good idea of the quality and craftsmanship of the builder's work. Make sure to speak to references as well, so you can assess if the builder was on-schedule and kept to the budget.

> Materials, labor, architectural fees, and permits generally run higher on islands, so research these costs and factor this in to your budget before you purchase property on an island or very remote area.

Particularly if you are not planning on being on-site every day to supervise work yourself, you must hire a construction manager to oversee the entire process. This can be someone from the building company you hire, or someone recommended by them. The construction manager's job is to ensure the building process is proceeding on schedule and on budget, and to manage the daily building activities on-site. Often, your contractor will serve as your construction manager and use a team of workers to do the physical labor. Regardless of whom you hire to manage the process, sit down with him or her before you break ground to list specifically what he or she will be responsible for.

6. Obtain a building permit. Before you begin construction, you must get a building permit from your town or city's Department of Public Works. After you have solidified construction costs, you will have to take the costs to the public works office and apply for the building permit. The permit is granted based on the projected cost of your construction, and the cost of the permit is also determined by your projected costs of construction. It is very important to present an accurate estimate of construction costs when applying for a building permit.

7. Determine the financial structure of the process. This is a very important step, as it will determine your budget for the entire project. Making sure that you and your contractor or architect are on the same page when it comes to finances is essential. There are two different ways to finance your project: Using a cost-plus approach, or a fixed-bid approach.

> **Cost Plus:** Taking a cost-plus approach means that you pay the contractor for all the materials and labor required on the project, plus an agreed-upon percentage on top of those costs. Typically, the percentage is around 15 percent but can be as high as 20 percent. According to "Before You Begin Construction" by Jeff Niemi, using this method means you are responsible for every single cost and payment to all employees, which includes paying the Social Security tax on each employee, and all other expenses. According to the article, if you use cost plus, you must be meticulous and able to manage the project closely.

> Using cost plus requires you to manage all the day-to-day finances and accounting. You will have to ensure that your contractor bills you for all expenses via a *factura* (invoice)

and that you keep all receipts to track your expenses. If you use the cost-plus structure, you will be paying a sales tax (the IVA tax) on every cost and labor, whereas if you use the fixed-bid structure, you will not be required to pay tax on your costs and labor.

Fixed Bid: Using a fixed-bid structure means you will determine a fixed cost at the beginning of the project that will include all materials and labor. Fixed-bid contracts are generally easier, as you do not have to manage so many details and provide funds for every cost that comes up. When using a fixed bid, the contractor is responsible for everything, which has its pros and cons. As long as you are using a reputable contractor whom you trust, going with a fixed bid is much easier. If you really want to control every detail and are on a tighter budget, using a cost-plus structure may be beneficial. Besides the ease of a fixed bid, you also will not be required to pay the IVA tax on every service and cost, although your contractor must still provides you with invoices on every payment.

In Mexico, there very minimal regulations or requirements a builder has to meet in terms of quality, which is something you should discuss with your builder before you begin construction to determine your expectations and make sure you are both on the same page.

8. Hire local, legal workers. You want to make sure that everything you do during the building process is legal and follows proper Mexican procedure. Hiring workers and managing their payroll is a big part of the process. If you hire workers through your architect or builder, they will likely manage the payroll process, but if you are hiring people yourself, you will be responsible for this. The typical workweek in Mexico is 48 hours, and you should ensure that every employee you hire is registered with the *Instituto Mexicano del Seguro Social* (IMSS), Mexico's Social Security system. Hiring an accountant to manage the financials of your project, which includes paying workers, is highly recommended, particularly if you are not familiar with managing finances.

9. Supervise the process yourself. The only way to ensure the progress and proper management of your project is to be there yourself every day to oversee the activity. Even if you hire a construction manager, you are opening yourself up to time and money delays if you decide to leave day-to-day management duties in someone else's hands. Being on-site every day will allow you to not only monitor progress and micro-manage all the details, but it will enable you to make sure no one is wasting valuable time and money. It also reduces the possibility that workers, electricians, architects, or anyone else you hire are doing their jobs in a timely fashion and within your budget. You are ultimately the only one who knows exactly what you want out of your home, and providing daily management and guidance is the way to make sure that it is what you get in the end.

10. Manifest your property. Determining how you will pay for your expenses and fund your project will be directly related to manifesting your property, which essentially means documenting your costs for the entire building process. For tax purposes, you will need to record every cost so the government can determine what it cost you to build your home.

According to "Before You Begin Construction" by Jeff Niemi, accurate manifestation is essential because you want the Mexican government to recognize your costs so you can deduct them on your taxes. Once you have completed construction, manifesting involves going back to the public works office with your building permit and your construction costs to get an official letter recognizing the end of your construction. The document is called the Letter of Termination of Works, and it will officially determine the cost of your property for tax and other purposes.

According to the same article, you will need to also pay Social Security tax on the labor used for your construction. Depending on which method you go with, either you or your contractor will be responsible for ensuring that these taxes are paid for day laborers and any other workers your hire throughout the process. The tax office will review receipts to verify that the proper amount of social security tax has been paid. When the amount is verified and deemed correct, the office will issue a Letter of Reasonability of Payment, and you will be cleared of any owed taxes. The necessity of keeping all your receipts throughout the construction process should be emphasized here, as you will need to refer to them if the tax office claims you did not provide proper payment.

The cost of construction you present to the public works office to obtain your building permit should match the actual costs that you present to the public works office at the end of construction to manifest your property.

CASE STUDY: EASY LAKESIDE LIVING

Jacque Jones had big ideas for her Mexican retirement home. A native Californian, Jones moved to Mexico permanently in 1987 with the intentions to build her dream home. After taking a drafting course in high school, she was determined to build a home instead of buy.

"It costs less, and I had my own ideas for a house plan," she said.

Armed with an adventurous spirit and a creative set of blue prints, Jones began the building process in 1992. She purchased a plot of land in a neighborhood of Lake Chapala, near Ajijic in the state of Jalisco, where utilities and other systems were already established. She chose the area for its laidback atmosphere and affordable living. With stores like Walmart and Costco nearby, and the Guadalajara airport less than an hour away, the Ajijic area offered a great balance of authentic Mexico and modern amenities. Puerto Vallarta is also accessible from Lake Chapala at just under four hours away.

Jones had her own building plans in mind.

"I hired an architect who copied my house plans but drew in the drainage system, about which I knew nothing," she said. "Plus, a licensed architect is required to present the plans for a building permit."

Working together with the architect, Jones drafted a blue print of her dream home. After her permits were cleared, a representative came to the site to verify the permit existed. She emphasized the importance of working with a licensed architect and acquiring all the right permits before you begin construction.

When it came time to hire workers, Jones used references from people she knew.

"Someone in my maid's extended family had built his home and had additional building experience, so I hired him as a foreman, and he selected helpers," she said. "I was my own contractor and had the foreman give me a list twice a week for materials needed. I paid the foreman and workers their wages, plus the required workers' insurance."

As for the building materials, Jones shopped around until she found a price and supplier she liked.

"I found a supplier who gave me contractors' wholesale prices so long as I agreed to purchase all materials from him," she explained.

The construction took about three months to complete. When construction was done, Jones had a one-story, 2-bedroom, 2.5-bathroom home with a large kitchen

---

CASE STUDY: EASY LAKESIDE LIVING

and living room, plus an area for a washer and dryer. She also created a large pantry for storage, a patio with a fountain, and a big garden with a variety of plants and landscaping, including a banana tree.

Overall, Jones described the process of building both easy and challenging.

"It was fun and an excellent way for someone with 'kitchen Spanish' to improve vocabulary," she explained.

Given the ideal climate in Lake Chapala, Jones has little need for air conditioning or heating, saving her money on electricity costs. Although she was retired when she moved to Mexico, Jones became an accountant for Mexconnect, an online magazine and resource center for all things Mexican, after she moved to the country, and has served as the magazine's accountant for ten years.

So what advice does Jones have for future builders? "Rent for six months to a year, look around, and ask questions," she said.

If she were to do it all over again, Jones would have used additional help when it came to managing workers.

"The workers' insurance is something I would turn over to a local accountant to handle should I ever build again, since it is time consuming, and there are too many possibilities for error."

For more information on Mexconnect, visit **www.mexconnect.com**.

What to Avoid When Building a Home

> ➢ **Beginning construction without a building permit.** This seems obvious, but still deserves mentioning for emphasis. Without a building permit, you will not technically be allowed to build on your property. If you begin construction without a building permit, you run the risk of stalling construction along the way and losing valuable time and money.

> ➢ **Applying for the building permit with a lower-than-actual cost of construction.** This is similar to registering the

appraised value of a house instead of the sales value to catch a break on the transfer tax. It all comes back to capital gains. When you sell your home, you must pay capital gains taxes unless you can prove you have used your home as a primary residence for at least two years. If your registered construction costs are significantly lower than the actual cost, you will end up paying more in capital gains. The government will see the difference — or the gain — between the registered cost of construction and the sale price and charge you capital gains on the difference, and you will end up paying taxes on money you never made.

➢ **Beginning construction without discussing quality expectations with your contractor.** Given that there are limited guidelines for quality when it comes to building in Mexico, you will have to determine the quality of a builder's work by visiting other buildings and development communities he or she has built. You should also discuss in detail what kind of craftsmanship you expect, including small details like moldings, light fixtures, and tiling. Being on the same page will help alleviate any differences in expectations that would otherwise arise during the process. You do not want to get halfway through construction to discover that the work quality is poor, or that the type of construction was different from what you expected.

➢ **Beginning construction without discussing financials with your contractor or architect.** You must sit down with you builder and determine if you will be taking a fixed bid or a cost-plus approach to managing the project. You do not want to be on a different page with your builder when it comes to finances because determining the financial structure will dictate the kinds of material and labor you will use, and it will also dictate your budget and what your contractor is specifically responsible for.

➢ **Beginning construction without a title or a trust.** This is similar to purchasing a home without the title. It is not recommended at all; if you do not have the title to the property you are planning to building on, it means you do not technically own that property, and anything you construct on it, you risk losing to the government. If you have not set up a trust with a Mexican bank, you should also not begin construction. Waiting until you have both the title and the trust is the best — and safest — way to approach building a home.

➢ **Ignoring the importance of manifestation.** In order for the government to recognize your property for tax purposes, you must manifest your home. Manifesting your home is equivalent to telling the government your home is finished and how much it cost to build. If you do not do this, and you ever sell the property, you could be faced with a big mess — not to mention a big headache.

The Advantages of Building

➢ **The ability to build your dream home in a hand-picked location.** Building a home can be a fun and creative process. Many people who choose to build in Mexico do so because they are looking for a custom-built home that they can create themselves from scratch.

> ➤ **The potential for a big profit.** If you do your homework and take time to research all your options, you can find some great deals on empty land. Especially if you are interested in a more remote area in a lower-profile location, finding afford- able land to build on is relatively easy. With low labor costs in Mexico and reasonably priced materials if you use the right ones, building a home can be very affordable. With the rapidly developing Mexican real estate market, the potential for turn- ing a nice profit if you decide to sell your home is enticing.

> ➤ **Going green.** Environmentally friendly homes are popular these days, as more people become conscious of the environ- ment and preservation. Going green is not just a great way to preserve the environment; it is a great way to reduce the cost of maintaining and running your home as well. Building a home from the ground up allows you to take advantage of some of the best and latest green building materials and en- ergy concepts to create an affordable, eco-friendly home. As the demand for eco-friendly homes rises, selling a modern, energy efficient, and eco-friendly home will give you a big advantage and the possibility for a nice profit.

The Disadvantages of Building

> ➤ **It can take a long time.** If you do not hire the right people — and even sometimes if you do — building a home can be a long and involved process. You will have to allow time and money in your budget for unexpected expenses, make sure you get all the right permits and clearances, and research a contractor or architect to manage the entire process. There is also a tendency in Mexico to work at a leisurely pace, so do

not expect things to get done as quickly as you may be used to in the United States.

> **The need for micro-management.** The best way to ensure the progress and the time and financial schedule of your project is to manage it yourself. Especially if you choose to use a cost plus financial structure, you will be required to manage every detail of the cost and labor. If you go with a fixed-cost structure, you will still want to manage the day-to-day work activity to ensure you get what you want in the end. With so much money and planning invested, it is only logical that you should also invest the time to see the project through on a daily basis.

> **Following rules and regulations.** Certain cities and towns have strict ordinances when it comes to building. Some do not allow fences and outside walls over a certain height, and others restrict the amount of property you can actually build on. Depending on where you build, you will have to research the ordinances and requirements and make sure your builder or contractor follows them throughout the process. Building rules and regulations may inhibit your building plans and require you to structure your design around the ordinances of the city.

Building New versus Remodeling

The option to purchase, remodel, and rework an existing home is an attractive option for certain buyers. If you want to avoid the process of designing a home, remodeling may be a great option. If you are looking to create a custom-built home, however, remodeling may not be the way to go, as remodeling a home is much more limited in what you can do than building a new one from the ground up. Certain parts of a home, like low ceilings, plumbing, and electrical systems, are difficult and can be expensive to improve or change. If you plan on creating an energy-efficient home, it is often easiest to build your own, as gutting a home and replacing the energy source, for instance, is no easy or inexpensive feat. If you want to do extensive renovations for aesthetic purposes while maintaining the original electrical and plumbing systems, renovating may be the best option.

Manufactured and Modular Homes

Mobile homes are popular in Mexico, as many high-end trailer and RV parks sit on beautiful beachfront lots and offer very affordable vacationing. Module homes, which cannot be transported like mobile homes, are also becoming more popular particularly for retirees. Developments and communities are offering more options for mobile home owners, as well as those interested in building a modular home.

By definition, a manufactured home is a trailer or mobile home. With so many gorgeous and luxurious mobile homes on the market, the initial concept of the mobile home and the reputation it carried for many years has shifted. Today, mobile homes offer all the amenities of an immobile residence and are an attractive option for many Mexican retirees and vacationers. Because mobile homeowners do not have to own land to enjoy the benefits of their mobile home, they are not obligated to some of a homeowner's responsibilities, like tending to landscaping, maintenance, and property payments like taxes. Mobile homes also travel easily and are great for a seasonal traveler or retiree. You can find a variety of RV parks throughout the country that have large communities of expatriates, vacationers, and retirees that offer very affordable services with nice amenities.

Modular homes, by contrast, are not mobile homes and are built in a factory and then transported to a land site. Modular homes are required to conform to all building codes particular to each geographical area. Built in sections in factories, modular homes offer a relatively custom-built home for an affordable price. There are several companies in Mexico that offer modular homes as well as communities and developments that allow modular homes. People who choose to purchase a modular home are usually doing so to enjoy an affordable second or retirement home, as opposed to an investment property.

Protecting Your Investment

When it comes to financing and protecting your investment, the process of building a home should be treated no differently than the process of purchasing a home. Your home should be treated as an investment, and sitting down with a financial advisor to determine a budget is crucial. Because building a home can be just as — if not more — costly than buying one, it is essential to define your limits and your expectations and consider the following:

> **The types of materials you want to build with.** This can make a big difference in your budget. For instance, if you want to use timber imported from out of the country or the highest quality marble and top-of-the-line appliances, expect to pay a lot more. Naturally, local materials are cheapest, but some people wish to use specific materials outside of Mexico. Expect to pay significantly more for any material you use that is not local to Mexico.

> **Your home-building timeline.** Drafting a timeline will determine how much labor you will require and for how

long, which will have a direct correlation to your budget. Why pay for labor that you are not going to need?

How you finance your construction. Financing is becoming much easier to obtain for foreigners purchasing real estate and land in Mexico. Obtaining a mortgage to finance your construction is a fairly simple process, and there are a variety of mortgage companies that specialize in cross-the-border mortgages that offer mortgages for people building homes.

As with purchasing a property, title insurance is an ideal way to protect your land investment. You will also want to purchase homeowner's insurance when your home is complete and make sure to manifest your construction costs to realize your profit when you decide to sell.

Building an Eco-Friendly Home

Eco-friendly homes are growing increasingly popular not only in Mexico, but around the world. Although green building is a fairly new concept, Mexico has taken advanced steps to recognize the significance, affordability, and advantages of building green.

The Mexican Green Building Council (MexicoGBC) is dedicated to sustainable and eco-friendly building and construction throughout Mexico. The council is a member of the World Green Building Council, which oversees the construction of green development on an international level. MexicoGBC has developed the Sustainable Building Rating Tool (SICES) to establish a green building standard on a national level. Visit their Web site at **www.mexicogbc.org** for resources and information on building an eco-friendly home.

From using solar power to installing energy-efficient windows, the options to create a sustainable home that is eco-friendly and cost-conscious are endless. Even if you cannot use some of the more advanced eco-friendly approaches to building, like solar power, doing things on a smaller scale will help you save money and will help the environment as well. For instance, using halogen lights instead of regular light bulbs will save energy *and* the cost you pay for it.

Taking an alternative approach to building your home requires a serious commitment to creating a system that works for you, and one that will actually benefit you and the environment. For instance, if you cannot commit to regulating your electricity use, then consider sticking to traditional energy sources and instituting smaller things you can manage, like recycling or using natural building materials for parts of your home.

When considering building an eco-friendly home, you want to avoid the "zero-sum" effect, which means negating the effects of alternative energy, materials, and processes by counteracting them. For instance, a zero-sum effect would be installing solar energy in your home but keeping electronics and appliances — like cell phone chargers — plugged in when you are not using them.

Building eco-friendly may be much easier than you think. The best way to approach the process is to analyze the natural resources around you, consider your location, and research what raw materials will be available. Doing so will optimize your eco-friendliness and enable you to use what is around you to make the process of building green as smooth as possible.

Using natural building materials and installing solar power in your home are two of the best ways to build an eco-friendly home in Mexico.

Using natural building materials

The use of natural building materials is an effective way of building an eco-friendly home. There are a variety of material options, and you should discuss the availability of materials with your builder. In general, eco-friendly homes use strong materials like concrete, stone, and adobe because these materials retain heat in the winter and keep interiors cool during the summer months. Using high-mass building materials like these will directly affect your heating and cooling costs, as these materials help balance the temperature in your home and protect it from the extreme heat or cold.

Within the category of high-mass building materials, there are a number of different varieties you can use. Depending on what is available in your specific location, you may want to consider using a high-mass material that will function in the same way as concrete or adobe but that offers more in terms of eco-friendliness. The following natural building materials are popular among eco-friendly homebuilders in Mexico:

> *Licensed timber.* Do not purchase wood from sources that are not regulated. In Mexico, using unlicensed wood is illegal; on top of that, it encourages deforestation and destruction of natural resources. Purchasing illegal timber only encourages illegal logging. If you decide to use timber, make sure the dealer is licensed to sell it. You can also find recycled timber in some areas of Mexico.

Compressed earth bricks. Compressed earth bricks are made from the earth's natural material, like clay, sand, and soil, and are created by compressing the material into a brick. Many of Mexico's buildings are also made of the similar high-mass combination of clay and sand, which forms a concrete-like material that is highly durable and great for maintaining temperatures.

Cactus-based paints. A popular alternative to lead and enamel-based paints are cactus-based paints, which are made with less chemicals and more natural materials. Like its name suggests, these paints are derived from the cactus plant. Cactus-based paints come in a variety of colors and work well with alternative building and high-mass materials, particularly earth bricks.

CASE STUDY: "RETIRE EARLY, RETIRE OFTEN"

When Suzanne Simmons and her husband first considered moving and retiring somewhere tropical and warm, they moved to Maui, Hawaii. From 1996 to 1999, the couple enjoyed Hawaiian living, but as the island became increasingly popular and touristy, the Simmons realized that the traffic and noise were not for them. "We turned our sights to Mexico," Simmons said, "and we knew within 45 minutes that this was the place for us."

The Simmons decided they wanted to build their home and bought a plot of land in Riviera Nayarit, about two hours north of Puerto Vallarta. The land they bought was in an existing development called Playa Las Tortugas.

"This is a unique place because it is remote, and we have a turtle conservation program on the beaches," Simmons said. The entire Playa Las Tortugas community is built on the concept of eco-friendly living, and Simmons and her husband decided to embrace the lifestyle.

The Simmons chose Riviera Nayarit to build their eco-friendly home. Well off the beaten path — and more than six miles from a main road — their land

CASE STUDY: "RETIRE EARLY, RETIRE OFTEN"

was located in an existing development, although very little building had been done. The developer already had title insurance on the land, and after they set up a trust with a bank and got a *fideicomiso,* the Simmons began the process of building. They found the purchasing process smooth, clear-cut, and quick. "It was extremely easy," Simmons said. "We had the luxury of interviewing all the homeowners here who had built, and we got the dos and don'ts."

In 2007, construction began. "Most people in Mexico buy with cash, but we took out a construction loan," explained Simmons, who added that the process of obtaining financing was fairly simple as well. She also used her community's developer — who was also the construction manager — as a resource, which proved to be a wise move. He took her ideas and initial drawings to three different architectural firms that bid on the project. With the Simmons' approval, the builder hired the architect that offered the most affordable services, and the process began. Simmons wanted to build green to reflect their commitment to the environment and to reflect their lifestyle. "It fit in with the value of what we do on this property, so we built green," she said.

Although the developer did not have much experience in using recycled and earth-friendly materials, he learned quickly, bringing in local materials and workers who were dedicated to getting the job done right. "So much in Mexico is built with cement and bricks," Simmons said. "We are in a hurricane-prone area, so we used compressed earth bricks to build. And since earth bricks breathe for many years, we could not use a latex paint, so we used a cactus-based paint for the house; you still get all the great colors."

With a little research and some help from local workers, the builder quickly learned how to work with compressed earth brick, and they began making the bricks on the property to use on the house.

Simmons spends her time enjoying the preserved ecosystems that thrive in Riviera Nayarit. The area is known for its sea turtle conservation program and whale- and bird-watching sites. "This is a very ecological friendly area here; the grounds are very beautiful," Simmons said. Her husband serves as the Development Director for the Platanitos Turtle Camp, "raising money, upgrading infrastructure, [and] enhancing programs."

When they first began building their home, there were only a handful of houses built in the area. Today, there are about 12 in her development — more than double the amount in only four years. As for advice to new builders, Simmons offers this:

Using Solar Power

Installing and using alternative energy sources in your home is the most effective way to reduce your carbon footprint and preserve energy — as well as money. Given Mexico's temperature and geographical location, using solar power as an alternative energy source is logical and accessible. Using Mexico's strong sun to create energy, solar power can be used to provide energy to many parts of your home. It can be used to provide electricity and light, and heat the water you use throughout your house.

Solar power works through the use of solar panels, which soak up the sun's energy and transfer it to energy that can be used in your home. The energy can then be used to heat hot water, offering an alternative to traditional oil and electric heating systems; it can also be used to provide electricity throughout your home. The sun can also provide natural light in your home, reducing the need for lamps and superficial lighting, and it can also be used for drying clothes as an alternative to electric dryers.

If you are considering building solar panels for electricity, you should hire an architect who is familiar with solar energy usage and can advise you on the design and structure of your home to get the optimal use of solar power.

Even if you are not installing and using solar panels, you can still make use of the sun to light and heat your home just by installing larger windows and skylights to face the direction of the sun. Although the sun's location changes throughout the day and according to season, the sun is the strongest mid-day, and installing windows and skylights facing south often allows your home to receive the most energy from the sun. Installing windows facing the sun will optimize the sun's presence in your home and help provide natural light and heat. On the other hand, reducing direct sunlight on certain areas of your home will help keep the interior cooler throughout the hot months.

In addition to solar power, wind power is another alternative energy source for your Mexican home. Although wind power in Mexico has traditionally not been used that much as an alternative energy source, the country is beginning to cultivate new ways to take advantage of it. A large wind farm was recently developed in Oaxaca, the largest of its kind in Latin America to date. The government has recently taken positive steps to reduce carbon emissions and preserve energy in the country.

Additionally, using recycled material is always a good way to conserve money and limit waste. Many homeowners in Mexico use bark as opposed to grass, plants, and flowers for their outdoor landscaping. These materials do not require much maintenance and can withstand the hot temperature, reducing the amount of water and pesticides used. If you have to use grass, using a salt-tolerant grass or one that can withstand direct heat with minimal water and shading can reduce water consumption as well.

PART III

The Process of Purchasing, Financing, and Securing Your Investment

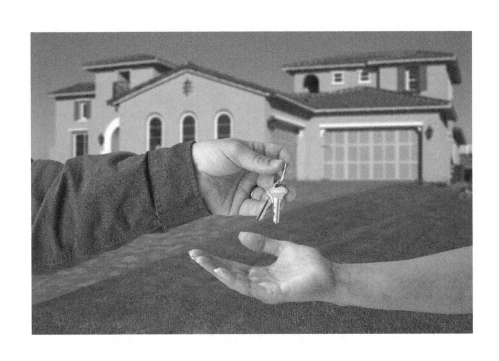

CHAPTER 9

The Process
of Purchasing

Once you have determined you are ready to buy property in Mexico, have carefully considered the financial obligations, and have chosen a specific property you want to make an offer on — whether is be a condo, timeshare, single-family home or empty plot of land — you are ready to begin the purchasing process. In a smooth transaction, where the title is clean and all permits are in order, the entire process can take as little as four to six weeks. Depending on where your property is located, how you are financing the purchase, what type of property, title status, *fideicomiso*, and all required permits, the process could take up to three months — or even longer.

There are two main problems that are the most common roadblocks to a smooth transaction:

- **Problems with the title or deed to a property.** Often, buyers — along with their real estate agent, lawyer, and financier — do not know that a complicated legal problem exists with the title until they are well into the process of purchasing. There are steps you can take to minimize the chances of title complications along the way, like hiring a closing agent or a title company to do a title search for you separate from the notario publico's review, but complications with titles usually get ironed out fairly quickly.

- **Hold-ups on the *fideicomiso* required for the restricted zone.** Delays can arise when the developer sells units without the ability to name the buyer as the beneficiary of the bank trust. Most often, this is because the developer is still in the process of establishing the condominium regime and has begun to sell units regardless. For you, the foreign buyer, this means that you cannot acquire title under the trust until the condominium regime is complete. Ensure that the developer has official approval from the government for the development, and that the condominium regime has been established before you sign any contract. In some cases, it is okay to sign a contract before the regime is officially established as long as it is almost complete. You should always seek the advice of a closing agent *before* doing so, however.

The process of purchasing has become much easier and smoother, but it still has a ways to come until it is foolproof. The best way you can ensure the process will go as smoothly as possible is to do your research, be involved with every step, and hire a good attorney familiar with Mexican law and real estate to guide you along the way. "Keep in mind the adage, 'If it sounds too good to be true, it probably is,' was invented for foreign ownership of real estate," warned Wayne Franklin of Tropicasa Realty.

The following purchasing steps and their order will vary slightly with each transaction and some are optional, such as hiring an independent appraiser to value your property and hiring a home inspector.

Step 1: Make an Offer and Negotiate the Best Deal

The offer initiates the purchasing process and sets the tone for the deal. It is also the first impression you are making to the seller, so your offer amount should be carefully considered with your agent. Making too low an offer can turn the sellers off, and they can reject your bid right away; making too high an offer can cost you money you do not necessarily need to spend. The key is determining a middle ground by consideration of the following factors:

- **The asking price.** Most properties are listed slightly higher than the seller expects to get for it. However, asking prices set the bar for the general price of the property. Depending on the market, you can make an offer that is 5-30 percent lower than the asking price. Be ready to negotiate with the seller.

- **The location and real estate demand.** The demand in the area plays a big role in determining your offer. With the global recession of 2008-09, many developers, retirees, and second homeowners put their properties on the market mainly to recover their financial losses. As demand for property diminished because of the lack of financial surplus most people experienced during this time, properties in some areas of Mexico were a dime a dozen. This gave those who *were* looking to buy — and had the means to do it — the upper hand when it came to negotiating, as many sellers were eager to unload their properties and therefore willing to accept offers lower than they would typically consider.

- **The market.** One of the best ways to analyze an offer on property is to do a comparable market analysis (CMA), where your real estate agent or an appraiser compares the selling prices of similar properties in the vicinity.

  You can create an analysis by simply understanding the real estate market in the particular area you are looking. Compare the asking price of properties with similar features, like square footage and amount of bathrooms and bedrooms. Where does the property you are interested in fall on the scale? If there are not many other similar properties for sale in the area, check other similar cities and towns. For instance, prices on oceanfront condos in gated communities are comparable for areas like Cancun, Puerto Vallarta, and some areas of Los Cabos. Being knowledgeable about the surrounding markets can be your most effective negotiating tool. A reputable appraiser can also provide these services.

- **How long the property has been on the market.** Often, if a property is on the market for more than a few months, the seller will consider lowering the price to attract more potential buyers. Determining how long the property has been on the market can determine how much leeway you have to make a low offer.

  Depending on the real estate market and the asking price of the property, if a house has been for sale for less than two weeks, there will be interest in it, and the seller may not will be not be as negotiable; so your offer should be around 5 percent below asking price. For properties on the market for two weeks to three months, offering 10-15 percent below asking price is acceptable in most circumstances, and if the property is on the market for more than three months, offering 20-30 percent below asking is reasonable.

- **Other interested buyers.** Competition drives up cost, and if your offer is competing against other offers, you will not have nearly as much negotiating room. Your real estate agent will be tuned in to whether other buyers are interested and when they make an offer. Although you will know if other buyers have made an offer, you will not know the amount they offer, which can work against you and for the seller. The best way to handle competing buyers and multiple offers is to set a limit for how much you are able to offer and then make a reasonably lower offer than your maximum. This will give you some room to negotiate and counter-offer.

- **How you are financing.** The majority of the properties purchased by foreigners in Mexico are purchased with cash. Paying with cash is attractive to sellers and can be a good negotiating tool because the process tends to go faster with cash, and the seller does not have to wait for the buyer's financer to approve a mortgage. If you are financing, which is becoming increasingly popular for Mexican purchases, getting pre-approved before you make an offer is another positive negotiating factor. This gives the seller security that you will be able to follow through on your offer. Financing can take almost double the amount of time to close as paying with cash, according to Wayne Franklin. Financing, he said, "can put you at a disadvantage when it comes to negotiating your dream home." Getting pre-approved, however, can cut this time down considerably.

Negotiating the Best Deal

You will most likely find the best deals in a seller's market in areas that are either overdeveloped or up-and-coming. However, this does not mean that you cannot find a great deal on a property that does not fall into one of these categories. Here are a few ways you can negotiate the best deal, no matter what type of property you are making an offer on:

- **Find out the seller's needs.** Naturally, if sellers are eager to sell their property, they will be more receptive to a lower offer. Finding out exactly what the seller wants — or, more importantly, how fast he or she is looking to sell — can give you the upper hand. During the 2008-09 recession many retirees and second home owners were forced to put their homes on the market for much less than they would normally list them for in a good economic environment. Properties like these have the most potential to offer great deals; looking particularly for these types of properties, which you can do best by asking around and talking to your realtor, can help you pinpoint the best deals in town.

  Similarly, developers are often the first people who are eager to sell when a real estate market goes bad because they have so many units and often must return some profit to survive in the market.

- **Sell yourself.** Mexican culture is all about relationships. Mexican people, and many of the foreigners whom you may be purchasing from, are generally warm and inviting, and having this demeanor as well can help you negotiate. Being standoffish and demanding will not get you anywhere, particularly in Mexico, where the majority of the people are friendly. Although the process of purchasing real estate is a business negotiation, there is also a personal side to it.

- **Get an appraisal.** Homes are often listed for more than they are worth, so getting an independent appraiser to calculate the value of the home can be a powerful negotiating tool. Companies like Montaña Verde offer valuation and appraisal services and environmental and market studies, which can save you thousands of dollars and prevent you from making an offer that is too high. By having an official appraisal to bring to the seller, you are letting the seller know that you have a very accurate understanding of the property's value.

   Enlisting valuation and appraisal services can also prevent you from making an offer on a property that has problems you are not aware of. A professional appraiser may identify key points about the property, like any environmental issues, that may lead you to believe that the investment is not a wise one.

Step 2: Sign the Offer to Purchase Contract

The contract for an offer is called an Offer to Purchase, and it essentially binds you to your offer; it is the first of three contracts you will sign throughout the process. The contract assures the seller that the buyer is serious about purchasing, and it assures the buyer that his or her offer is accepted, and he or she will be able to purchase the property.

Once the Offer to Purchase has been made, and the seller has accepted the offer in writing and both parties have signed the paperwork, the property should be taken off the market. Before you sign, you should review the contract carefully to understand all stipulations, which should include:

- **A time limit for the seller to review and accept your offer.** This prevents the process from becoming overly long and enables all parties to either proceed to the next step or end the process before any money or significant time has been invested.

- **The description of the property.** The Purchase-Sales Agreement will detail this further, but the Offer to Purchase should include at least a minimal description of the property and where it is located.

- **The details of an escrow deposit.** This includes the name of the escrow company you will be using, or if you are using a real estate agent or closing agent, it will include their name and contact information.

- **The earnest money requirements.** An earnest money deposit, which will go into an escrow account, is not always refundable if the buyer defaults, so you may wish to include a clause that entitles you to a refundable earnest money deposit — within a limited period — should you decide to rescind or if certain conditions of the Offer to Purchase contract are not met. If a refundable deposit is not possible, a penalty for a lesser amount of the deposit may be.

It should be noted that some transactions do not use an Offer to Purchase, like those taking place outside the restricted zone. The purpose of the agreement is to bind the offer while the rest of the details are worked out. Since property in the restricted zone requires research and a *fideicomiso*, the process tends to be longer, and it benefits both parties to use a promissory agreement to prevent the deal from falling through in that time.

Some less formal transactions use verbal offers, but it can be risky because you are not protected by a contract, and the deal could fall through at any point. You should always make sure your contracts are in Spanish, but also have an English translation included. You are entitled to review the Spanish contract before signing it to ensure that the translation is accurate and you understand all the terms.

Step 3: Deposit Your Money in Escrow

The introduction of escrow services in Mexico has vastly changed the process of purchasing property by providing protection for buyers. In the 1990s, American-based title company Stewart Title Guaranty, with the help of Snell Real Estate, began offering title insurance and escrow services to those purchasing property in Mexico.

Although Mexican-based escrow companies do not exist, and there are currently no government regulations on escrow services in the country, U.S. title companies like First American Title, Stewart Title Guaranty, and The Settlement Company specialize in international real estate purchases. Select banks and credit institutions in Mexico, along with some real estate agencies and attorneys, also offer escrow services.

The best way to ensure your funds are secure and protected is to deposit them in a U.S., FDIC-insured escrow account. If you are using a closing agent, he or she will provide instructions on where and when to transfer the funds. Using an attorney, a real estate agent, or even a regulated Mexican bank for escrow services provides little security because of the lack of government regulation and licensing. U.S. companies place your funds into protected accounts that can generate interest, if requested, making you money while it sits in escrow.

Exactly when you deposit your money into escrow funds and how much you will deposit can vary. Typically, the amount put into escrow is typically 10-20 percent of the sale price of the property, but can be as much as half, depending on the transaction. Money is deposited into escrow when both parties sign the Offer to Purchase.

In some transactions, the buyer will be required to make a small earnest money deposit — put into escrow — to initiate the Offer to Purchase and then put a larger portion of the sale price into an escrow account after both parties sign the offer. "Even if [the escrow money] is non-refundable if the buyer defaults, it is always refundable if the seller defaults," Chris Snell said. That is a stipulation to protect the buyer if the seller rescinds and decides to terminate the process.

"Make sure you keep your money in a U.S. escrow account until you get title, and make sure you get your title *before* you release your money to the seller," Snell added.

Escrow funds should only be released to the seller after you have signed the deed for the property, the title has transferred to your name, and you have received the keys to your home. This should be clear to the seller in the contract. Releasing funds before you receive the deed, title, and keys is risky and increases the chances you will lose your escrow money, should something go wrong.

Step 4: Sign the Promissory Agreement

The Promissory Agreement is another preliminary contract that establishes the intent of both parties to eventually sign a Purchase-Sales Agreement and transfer title to the new owner. Like the Offer to Purchase, the Promissory Agreement confirms that the buyer and seller will proceed to the next step while the details are worked out. If you are purchasing a pre-construction unit, the contract is often referred to as a Reservation Agreement, or a Promise to Trust contract, because you are reserving a particular unit in a development.

The Promissory Agreement must be in writing and should detail the following, but can include more information depending on the transaction:

- The full names of both buyer and seller

- The bank that will issue the trust or transfer the trust to the new owner

- The conditions of the Purchase-Sales Agreement

- The price of the offer

- A projected date that the Purchase-Sales Agreement will be signed

The agreement has three different versions to specify three different types of transactions:

- A promise to transfer title

- A promise to complete a sale

- A promise to transfer rights of a real estate trust

Your real estate agent and closing agent will advise you which contract the sale will use; it will depend on a variety of things, including if the property is already in a trust and the trust will be transferred to you, or if a trust needs to be established. If you are purchasing a property from a developer, it is important to do several things at this stage, including:

- Review the condo regime and all association fees

- Ensure the developer has legal title

- Ensure the developer will transfer the trust to you at the time of purchase if the property is in the restricted zone

It is important to note that like all contracts, you should review the Promissory Agreement with a lawyer or closing agent before you sign to make sure there are no hidden clauses that will benefit the seller at your cost. No funds should be transferred at this point. If you transfer funds to the seller at this time and do not wait until the title is obtained and the trust is established, you will risk losing your deposit if it is discovered that the seller does not hold the title to the property and is unable to transfer it to you.

There is also the possibility that the government will officially recognize the sale of the property with the exchange of escrow funds, and you will be responsible for paying taxes starting at that point. If you technically purchase the property by releasing escrow funds to the seller and do not realize you are obligated to pay taxes, you could face serious monetary penalties.

Step 5: Initiate the Trust Application

After the promissory agreement has been reviewed and signed by both parties, you should begin the process of obtaining a bank trust or transferring an existing trust if your property is in the restricted zone. As the buyer, you are responsible for initiating this step and for ensuring that the details are carried out appropriately, but will most likely enlist a closing agent to perform these services. The steps to establishing a trust include the following:

- Establishing if a trust needs to be set up or whether an existing trust will be transferred to you

- Contacting the bank you will be using for your trust to initiate the process

- Obtaining the *Secretaría de Relaciones Exteriores* (SRE or Secretary of External Relations) permit from the Ministry of Foreign Affairs of Mexico. This is something the bank and closing agent will do, but you are responsible for ensuring it has been completed. You must get approval via this permit in order to establish a *fideicomiso*

- If the seller is transferring the title to you, notify the bank and the Ministry of Foreign Affairs

- Designating beneficiaries

"It is important to note that anybody can be your beneficiary," Wayne Franklin said. "They do not have to be blood relatives."

If you are purchasing property that is already held in a trust, you may not be required to get a new trust; you can often simply have the rights of the existing trust transferred to you. You may, however, want to weigh the benefits of establishing a new trust. According to Linda Neil, "When considering a new trust or an assignment of rights, the factors to be considered are: 1) Remaining term of the existing trust — when will it need to be renewed? 2) What are the annual bank fees under the existing trust? If the permit has an unexpired term of less than fifteen or twenty years and the annual bank administration fees are more than $500, it probably makes sense to obtain the permit for a new 50-year trust with a bank offering more attractive fees."

Just like mortgage rates and terms, bank fees and terms for trusts change often, so it is in your best interest to evaluate what will save you the most money and time. Although transferring a trust may seem easier now than applying for a new one, it may not be the best option long term, as you may be able to lock in a great annual fee at the time of your purchase. "Over the past few years, there has been a substantial decrease in annual fees, and it makes sense to shop around for the most favorable rate for the property being purchased if a new trust is contemplated," Neil advised.

Step 6: Conduct the Title Search and Obtain Title Insurance

It is the *notario publico's* job to review the No Lien Certificate and to draft the deed for transfer to the new buyer. However, the *notario* cannot be held accountable if there is a problem with the title, and he or she often does not do a full search on the title that includes its entire history; their research often goes back only a few years. This can present problems down the road if a glitch is discovered that prevents you from being able to obtain use your property. Although *notarios* are highly regarded, some, depending on whom you use, do more extensive searches on the title than others.

Title search companies will conduct a more thorough investigation and produce a history of ownership. At Snell Real Estate, title searches, done through Stewart International title company, search the history of the property all the way back to the Mexican Revolution. A search this extensive is sure to turn up any issues that exist and enable the buyer to be aware of these issues early in the purchasing process.

Title problem scenario No. 1: A buyer puts an offer on a single-family home that was built 20 years ago. The home has since been bought and sold twice, and you would be the third owner. When the initial owner built the home, he did not get the proper city and state building permits and clearances, and never properly manifested his property. Because he never manifested his property correctly — either by intention or not — the amount of the property's worth is incorrectly stated to the government, and none of the previous owners have been paying proper taxes. Until the government irons out any back taxes and works out the building permits, you will not be able to purchase the property because the seller does not have the right to transfer the title to you. Only a thorough title search that investigates more than one or two owners ago will turn up such an issue.

Title problem scenario No. 2: You put an offer in on a one-bedroom condo in a gated development community in a popular beachside town. You check to ensure the developer has legal title and the *notario's* review of the No Lien Certificate validates that the title is clear. You confirm with the developer that the trust can be transferred to you when you purchase. Three years after you purchase your condo, someone buying a condo in your development hires a title company to do a more in-depth search before a purchase, and it is discovered that the land was once *ejidal* land that was never properly privatized or registered. The title to the plot of entire land — part of which is not in your name — is now compromised as the nature of the land is disputed in court. Even though the *notario's* search did not indicate any problems with the title, and you took all the precautionary measures to ensure the developer had the legal right to transfer title to you at the time, you now risk losing your home if the courts decide that the developer never had the right to develop on the land at all. Situations like this are rare, but do happen.

In other words, it is best to order a full-title investigation through your closing agent. Hiring a title company to do this can cost around $500 to several thousand dollars, but is often well-worth the money; plus, it decreases the chances of a faulty title causing major hold-ups in the purchasing process. Many title companies offer multiple services, making it easy to consolidate all your needs into one company. The Settlement Company, for instance, offers title search, title insurance, escrow, and closing services. The Settlement Company, Stewart Title Guaranty and Fidelity, and First American Title are three of the biggest companies offering title insurance to foreign investors.

If you mortgage a property, your lender may require a more in depth title search in order to grant you the loan. In this case, this is another layer of protection for you, and it may not be necessary to hire an independent title search on your own; this may be conducted by your mortgage company anyway and included in the process of obtaining a loan. Make sure to ask your mortgage company if they will conduct a more thorough title search.

The Importance of Title Insurance

At this point, you should also purchase title insurance. The process begins with a title search, which your title insurance policy holder will conduct. The company will then produce a Preliminary Title Report detailing the history of the title. If you are mortgaging a property, your financier will most likely require a title insurance policy. If you are paying with cash and are not involving a financer, obtaining title insurance on your own is highly recommended to protect your purchase.

Even though a *notario* may produce a clean title, and even if you get approved for a bank trust, you are still not protected if a problem with the title arises down the road, which can mean at the end of the purchasing process or in ten years. As you have read in previous sections, there have been stories of buyers losing their homes after problems with title were discovered years after they purchased. The insurance takes effect when you close on your property, and the deed has been signed to you.

According "Do I Need to Obtain Title Insurance For the Purchase of My Mexico Real Estate?" by Matthew A. Miller, "As in the U.S. and Canada, title insurance serves as a 'contract of indemnity' that protects the insured purchaser against any loss due to a defective title. It is important to note that a *fideicomiso* does not replace title insurance. (A *fideicomiso* can be invalidated if any prior claims, liens, and encumbrances surface.) When purchasing title insurance, it is important to carefully review the master policy for any limitations or exclusions. It is imperative to confirm the policy covers the property's land, not just the *fideicomiso*."

Title insurance from a U.S. insurance company offers the same protection as it offers to U.S. homeowners; it protects you against monetary damages if the title proves to be invalid or defective during the process of transferring it, which includes the scenarios previously discussed in this section. In general, title insurance will protect you from monetary damages as a result of:

- Unforeseen and undisclosed liens on the property, which can include things like tax liens, labor fees owed to a contractor, and homeowner's association fees owed if the property is in a condominium

- The discovery that your property is *ejidal* land that was never properly privatized

- Contracts that are discovered to be invalid, which can be a result of forgery, a signature by an invalid power of attorney, or a signature from someone who does not have legal right to sign (such as someone under the age of 18)

- A transaction that is deemed invalid or unauthorized. Unauthorized transactions can include the improper registration of your property with the Public Registry of Property or the issuance of a deed that does not bear the official stamp of the Public Registry

- The discovery that the seller did not hold legal title to the property and never had the right to transfer it you

In general, title insurance policies do *not* cover:

- Defaults on a mortgage payment

- Any monetary penalties incurred as a result of a buyer's non-compliance with Mexican law, including zoning, environmental, and building regulations

- Any defects that are your fault, like damage to your property

- Theft, fire, flooding, or any other similar occurrence. A good homeowner's insurance policy will protect against events like these

In the event that any of these situations occur, your title insurance company will pay all costs associated with the dispute. Developers should have a title insurance policy for the entire development, and individual buyers can obtain a separate policy for their single unit as well.

Step 7: Obtain the Necessary Documents

There are a variety of documents and certificates you will be required to produce before the government will officially recognize your final contract. At this stage, you should be serious about purchasing and going through with the final contract. If you are not, now is the time to end the process.

While the Ministry of Foreign Affairs is processing the trust permit, you will need to obtain the following list of documents. After the ministry approves your permit, you will be required to pay for the *Registro Nacional de Inversiones Extranjeras* (RNIE) fee, which is for the registration of your deed in the National Foreign Investment Registry.

You as the buyer are responsible for ensuring you have each certificate to present to the *notario*, who will oversee your title transfer and verify your Purchase-Sales Agreement. The *notario* will not proceed to closing until these certificates have been provided and verified.

Although sellers can provide most documents, they may not have them readily available or up-to-date. This can add some time to the process as the realtor and attorney track down the certificates or get new copies from the Public Registry of Property.

The Certificate of No Encumbrances

The Certificate of No Encumbrances ensures that there are no liens on the property. A property can have liens because of a variety of owed funds to previous builders, the government, or creditors. You do not want to inherit the seller's debt; obtaining this certificate is an important step that will prevent this.

The Certificate of No Tax Liability

The Certificate of No Tax Liability does exactly what it seems: It provides official assurance that there are no taxes owed on the property. It also serves as a back up of sorts to the Certificate of No Encumbrances and provides a more in-depth view of the tax history of the property. If the seller owes any taxes, they must be paid in full before he or she can transfer title to you.

Additional Requirements

You may be required to provide an additional number of certificates and documents depending on your transaction and where your property is located. Requirements can vary from state to state, and your attorney and real estate broker will advise you what the municipal and state rules are for your particular area. The *notario* working on your transaction will request the necessary documents, as he or she will be familiar with the specific requirements of the state in which your property is located.

Just as a *notario* cannot guarantee your title, he or she cannot guarantee the certificates, either. Even though the lien certificates are acquired from the Public Registry of Property, many times these certificates only date back a few years and do not reveal tax or other liens on the property that have previously existed and were never settled. This is another reason to hire a title company to do an extensive search on the history of the property for you and provide you with title insurance.

Additional certificate requirements the *notario* may request before closing can include a property appraisal and land valuation, a certificate stating your land is not *ejidal*, a Certificate of No Water Debt, and a certificate verifying the acquisition tax has been paid.

Step 8: Get a Property Appraisal and a Land Survey

Getting an official property appraisal and a survey of the land is one of the required steps to setting up your bank trust. It establishes the value of your property and your land, and ensures that the property is in accordance with zoning regulations. According "Purchasing Your Dream Home in Mexico" by Linda Neil, "The appraisal must be made by an appraiser who is usually an architect and who is recognized as a *perito valuador*, an official appraiser, by the property tax authorities in the municipality where the property is located." Usually an appraiser will be an attorney legally licensed in Mexico. However, it is possible that the bank with whom you are setting up your trust and is acting as your trustee will provide the appraisal.

The appraisal is for the government to establish the value of your property to decipher your future tax obligations. The official appraiser assigned to assess the value of your home for tax purposes should not be confused with an independent appraiser, also referred to as a commercial appraiser, whom you may hire at the beginning of your purchasing process to provide you with an accurate appraisal of the property for negotiating purposes. The appraisal from the government is mandated, while the commercial appraiser is not.

The appraiser will provide the *notario* with the proper information and verified certificates. Your tax payments will be based on whichever is higher: the sales price of the property or the tax appraisal. The appraised value of property is often lower than the sale price, which is another indicator that hiring a commercial appraiser to value the property before you make an offer is a good idea. This commercial appraisal, however, has no bearing on your tax obligations.

Step 9: Get a Home Inspection

This is an optional step, but one that you would be wise to take, as it can provide you with more protection. A home inspector is responsible for providing a detailed report that speaks to the soundness of your property's structure. If there are any issues with any major functions of the home, the inspector will reveal them. In addition to smaller things like smoke detectors, appliances, and light fixtures, a home inspector will review the following that are the more serious aspects of a property:

- The foundation

- The electrical wiring and plumbing

- The roof and floors

- The construction of walls

- The heating and cooling systems

- Water pipes and draining systems

- Any chimneys or fireplaces

Home inspectors are not licensed in Mexico, and they can sometimes be hard to come by. Depending on your property's location, you may be able to find an independent inspector like Brad Grieve, who inspects homes in the Ajijic area and advises clients on the home's issues before they purchase.

According to Bruce Greenberg of Montaña Verde, although there are not that many home inspectors in Mexico, the service is valuable, and buyers can look for a licensed architect in their geographical area who can serve as a home inspector. The other option, he noted, is to bring in a licensed home inspector from the United States to do this service. If you are unable to do this, your real estate agent or your Mexican attorney should be able to provide a recommendation for either a home inspector or a licensed architect in the area.

If you are getting a home inspection on a property you have made an offer on, your purchase-sales contract should include a clause that subjects the deal to a positive home inspection. You should also negotiate the terms of your escrow money to be refundable, should the home inspector uncover significant damages to or issues with the property. This will protect you from losing your escrow funds.

Step 10: Do a Final Walk Through

This is an important step and should not be overlooked, even if you hired a home inspector. Doing a walk through will ensure that everything is intact on the property, all systems are working, and the home is in the condition it was in when you made your offer.

A walk through should be done as close as possible to the closing date. It is most beneficial to do them after the previous owners have moved out, although this is not always possible. The walk through is something you should do yourself, but you can include your realtor for back up. It can take as little as an hour to do — or longer, depending on the size of the property — and making a checklist of what needs inspection is highly beneficial. You should check the functionality of the following during a walk through:

- Faucets, toilets, showers, and all other sources of water, including outside sprinklers.

- All lights and electrical outlets.

- Cable and telephone jacks.

- Windows and doors.

- Air conditioning units and ceiling fans.

- Garage doors and all appliances.

- Heating systems.

You should ensure there are no holes in any walls, especially in closets and behind doors, and there are no cracks in the floors or walls. You should also look outside to check the landscaping, windows, sprinkler system, gutters, roof, and door. If you are purchasing a unit in a development, check that the common areas, the pool, and all outside light fixtures are functioning properly.

Step 11: Sign the Deed Before the Notary and Close on the Property

The last of three contracts is the final contract, which is signed before the *notario publico*. This contract legally transfers the title to you, the new owner. If the property is located within the restricted zone the contract will be with the bank holding the *fideicomiso*. If the property is located outside the restricted zone, the contract is called a Purchase/Sale Contract. Either way, the seller signs the deed to place the title in the name of a Mexican bank, or grants it fee simple to the buyer if the property is not in the restricted zone and does not involve a *fideicomiso*.

The final contract will include, at minimum, the following:

- The names of both parties

- A description of the property, which includes lot size, dimensions, and location

- The purchase price

- If the property is in the restricted zone, the bank trust information, which includes the details of the trust and the name of the bank holding the trust

If you have hired a home inspector, you should not sign the deed until the inspection has taken place and any necessary improvements have been made to the property. At this stage, the *notario* will witness the signing between both parties and provide you with the deed; this will officially transfer title to you.

After you have completed all the requirements and the *notario* has all the needed paperwork in order, the document is signed by all parties. This can be done personally or through a power of attorney issued to your closing agent.

Neil explained the next step: "Upon signature by all parties, the notary public files a notification with the Public Registry that the transfer has taken place. He or she will pay the appropriate taxes and record the document. It generally takes two to three months to complete this process after which your closing agent should provide you with your deed; a brief translation of the deed, and an audited accounting of all funds received and paid out on your behalf, with a check for any overage."

Clarifying Misconceptions

There are several misconceptions about the closing process and what it costs that need clarification.

Misconception No. 1: The closing process in Mexico is lengthy, confusing, and full of hold-ups, particularly when a transaction involves a mortgage lender. Matthew A. Miller explained, "This has some merit historically when mortgages were first rolled out several years ago and each lender and broker was figuring out the process, but is not currently an accurate assessment." Today, the closing process is much more streamlined, and lenders like ConfiCasa Mortgage International are very knowledgeable about the process and can even make the process smoother and easier to understand.

Misconception No. 2: High closing costs offset the reasonable real estate. Closing costs *are* higher in Mexico than they are in the United States, but this evens out with the very low cost of living and owning in Mexico in the form of low property taxes, if you will be long-term owning. "Real estate taxes are in the hundreds of dollars per year in Mexico, rather than thousands like in the United States, so this mitigates the 2 percent transfer tax and higher closing costs up-front," explained Miller.

Misconception No. 3: Closing costs are much higher if you use a lender and do not pay with cash. Miller explained: "Fees in Mexico are significantly higher than in the U.S and Canada for *both* cash purchases and financed purchases, and most of them are set fees and not negotiable." Certain well-known lenders in the Mexican real estate industry do have the power to negotiate certain rates and fees for you, which can lessen your overall closing costs.

Misconception No. 4: You have to be present at the closing, and that means flying to Mexico. Given the nature of Mexican purchases as investment and second properties, many buyers take advantage of the fact that they do *not* have to be present at closing. You must, however, assign a Power of Attorney to your closing agent to sign on your behalf, regardless of the type of property you are purchasing.

Misconception No. 5: The cost of a mortgage for a Mexican property is extremely high. Miller explained this misconception: "A borrower pays the full cost of the loan at closing for a Mexico mortgage as compared to spreading the costs over the life of the loan through higher interest payments," which is the case for most mortgages for properties in the United States. "Mexico second home mortgages charge fees on the front end through loan origination points. First and second home mortgages in the United States sometimes charge up-front points, but more likely charge their fees as part of the interest rate, known as 'yield spread premium,' [explained further in Chapter 10]." Therefore, it is more difficult to see the true costs of a second home mortgage in the United States, but often they are equal or often even greater than that of a Mexico mortgage.

Closing Costs and Fees

Typically, the buyer is responsible for the following closing costs:

- The transfer/acquisition tax

- The cost of all the certificates of liens

- The bank trust fee

- The permit fees

- The *notario's* fees

- The tax appraisal fee

- Closing agent fees, if you are using one

- Title insurance and title report fees

- Escrow fees

- Home inspection fees

- Buyer's attorney's fees, if you are using one

The seller is responsible for:

- Capital gains tax

- The real estate agents' commissions

- Seller's attorney fees

The following chart is based on fee averages for closing costs, provided in part by ConfiCasa Mortgage International. Rates change frequently and vary from state to state. You should always confirm costs prior to initializing the process, as the below fees are only estimates and vary by region and purchase price; costs can also depend on what closing agents, *notarios*, title companies, or other third parties you enlist during the process. If you are going to mortgage your property, you can add about 3 percent of the price of your mortgage, which must be paid up-front on many mortgages on international properties, plus a commercial appraiser fee of $1,200 to $1,500; your lender will require both.

Service/Certificate:	Cost:
Fideicomiso	
-Initial set-up fee	$1,500
-Annual fee	$500
-Registration fee	Up to .5 percent of the sales price
Notario publico	$1,000-$3,500
Ministry of Foreign Affairs Permit (SRE) & Foreign Investment Permit (RNIE)	$1,800 for both
Home inspection (optional)	$500
Certificate of No Liens	Under $100
Certificate of Property Taxes	Under $100
Acquisition tax	2 percent of the sale price

Service/Certificate:	Cost:
IVA (Sales) tax	10-15 percent of the price of services provided by the *notario*, appraiser, home inspector, and any other service provider.
Tax appraisal	.15-.20 percent of the sale price
Closing agent (optional)	$1,500-$2,500
Escrow (optional)	$500-$1,500
Title Insurance -Preliminary title report and investigation -Title insurance	$500-$3,000 Averages $6-$7 per $1,000 of the purchase price. You will also pay a 15 percent sales tax.
Power of Attorney (optional)	Up to $300

CHAPTER 10

Financing
Your Investment

Traditionally, the second home market in Mexico has been a 95-98 percent cash market for four main reasons: 1) The typical home buyer for these markets is purchasing property for investment, retirement, or vacation purposes; 2) Most of these buyers have the funds to purchase from their 401(k)s, IRAs, their recently vested stocks and bonds, the sale of another home, or from a home equity line; 3) The lack of mortgaging options in Mexico for foreigners; and 4) The high interest rates offered by the limited amount of Mexican lenders who do offer financing for a second or retirement home in Mexico.

The purchasing market in Mexico has grown tremendously in the past decade, and along with that growth has come an increase in options for financing a purchase. "When the market was more immature, paying with cash was the only option. However, demand for alternative funding sources increased as buyers without the adequate liquid assets or desire for financing options increased significantly," Matthew A. Miller explained. The addition of mortgages to the pool of financing options has opened up the market to a whole new category of people who may not have all the cash available up front to purchase property or just prefer to finance their purchase.

Because mortgaging a Mexican property is becoming increasingly popular and there is limited information available on mortgaging in Mexico, this chapter will concentrate mostly on mortgages and touch on other financing options at the end of the chapter.

Mortgaging Your Property

In the past, mortgages had been rarely used in Mexico, especially by foreign buyers, but that has changed dramatically over the past few years. More and more lenders are tapping into the growing purchasing market in Mexico and offering buyers a variety of financing services. Most lenders that offer financing are specialized U.S. mortgage companies that are well-versed in the process of purchasing in Mexico specifically. Companies like ConfiCasa Mortgage International offer mortgages that cater to a variety of different buyers, types of properties, and price ranges.

In addition to interest rates, variation of loans offered, and flexibility, one of the most important factors when choosing a lender is their closing history. According to "What Product Features Should Be Considered When Seeking a Mexico Mortgage Loan" by Matthew A. Miller, "Each direct lender or indirect lender should be able to provide a history of closings." The history can give you an idea of how successful the lender has been in closing deals, and it can "assure that your dream property will become a reality."

The Benefits of Mortgaging Your Mexican Property

You do not have to tap into retirement and savings funds. It used to be that if you did not have the ability to take out a home equity line of credit, use your IRA, or cash in stocks or bonds, you were out of luck if you wanted to purchase a home in Mexico. With mortgage financing options, buyers can limit the need to tap into retirement and savings funds and can instead leave this money in the bank to collect interest and use for the future. It also opens the door for people who may not have enough cash to fund an entire purchase but who only have a small portion for a down payment. Additionally, the market crash of 2008-2009 has gravely reduced opportunities to cash in on IRAs and 401(k)s, and to take out a home equity line of credit on an existing residence.

Adjustable interest rates. If you do your homework, you will find a handful of international mortgage companies that offer adjustable interest rates. Especially if you go with a short-term mortgage, you can expect the rates to be more in your favor because you will be paying back the loan in a shorter period of time.

Your interest may be deductible. If you are a U.S. citizen, the interest you pay on your mortgage can be deducted from your annual taxes. According to "What Are the Benefits in Obtaining Mexico Mortgage Financing for My Mexico Dream Home?" by Matthew A. Miller, "Mortgage interest paid on a primary or secondary home is tax deductible in the U.S. up to $1 million ($500,000 if you are married but filing separately). The [IRS] publication does not specify whether the house must be located in the U.S., which enables deductions to be applied to your financed Mexico property." You should, however, remember to consult with a tax attorney before making a purchase using mortgage financing to ensure that the interest is in fact deductible.

Funds are in dollars versus pesos. The exchange rate can vary significantly, and this can affect the cost of your mortgage greatly if you pay in pesos. With U.S. lenders offering financing on Mexican properties, your loan will be in dollars. This prevents any significant decrease in the value of the peso from losing you money during the process or when you sell your property and pay back the loan.

Security and guidance. Although buying with cash is much more secure in Mexico now than it was in the past, there is still a slight risk you take with using cash, especially if you are not smart about taking precautionary measures or are not aware of them. With a mortgage, you can feel 100-percent secure in knowing that your lender is just as invested in your property as you are. Because of this, lenders will make sure that the title investigation, trust application, and all other processes are followed properly, and that the property is clear of any liens. After all, they want to make sure your process is legitimate because they are taking the risk of financing the purchase. In the end, lenders want to make money also, and this involves ensuring your purchase is solid and the process thorough.

Why Requirements Are More Stringent For Mexico Mortgages

There are several reasons why mortgages for Mexican properties require higher down payment amounts than in the United States and offer slightly higher interest rates. In "Clarifying Many Misconceptions," Matthew A. Miller explained three reasons why costs are higher for mortgages on Mexican properties: "First, lenders offering cross-border Mexico home financing programs are U.S. and international finance institutions lending in a foreign country's second and retirement home markets. While we (and you) already know that Mexico's resort markets are a safe place and have huge potential ... they are still different than the U.S. or Canada and, therefore, some incremental risk does exist."

Secondly, "the financial institutions that underwrite these loans hold onto the loans as opposed to packaging them and selling them in the secondary market. Further, government agencies who purchase and guarantee such mortgages (like Fannie Mae and Freddy Mac in the United States) do not exist for Mexico mortgages," Miller added. While these factors require lenders to raise rates and minimum down payments for Mexican purchases in order to mitigate risk of holding the loans, you are ultimately much more protected as a buyer. "While higher interest rates and higher down payments may be a bit tougher to swallow, they are good news for the Mexico real estate market, as they mitigate many of the risk factors seen in the U.S. and will help ensure that the Mexico mortgage and real estate market thrives for a long time" he explained.

Lastly, the concept of yield spread premium (YSP) can explain the higher up front costs on a mortgage for a property in Mexico. "The yield spread premium is the cash rebate paid to a mortgage broker based on selling an interest rate above the wholesale rate for which the borrower qualifies," Miller explained. In other words, while the interest rate for a mortgage on a U.S. property may seem very low, there are often built in costs that are difficult for the buyer to see. "More specifically, the interest rate the mortgage company offers the borrower in the U.S. is not the lowest rate for which the buyer qualifies. The incremental difference in interest rate is how U.S. mortgage lenders are able to make money. This concept is not often understood by the borrower," he added.

"In many cases, U.S. mortgages that include an added interest (through the notion of the YSP) may cost more over the life of the loan than a cross-border Mexico mortgage, which only charges points up-front," Miller said. "The difference of the two is that a borrower pays the full costs of the loan at closing for a Mexico mortgage as compared to spreading the costs over the life of the loan through interest payments for a U.S. mortgage."

One of the main differences when you use mortgage financing to purchase property in Mexico's restricted zone as opposed to paying with cash or alternate funding is the use of the *fideicomiso de garantía* as opposed to a regular *fideicomiso*. The *fideicomiso de garantía* simply puts the lender in first position on the trust; if the borrower defaults on the mortgage, the lender is protected. Your lender will work with the *notario* to complete the required paperwork, which does not differ much from the regular trust paperwork used for a cash purchase.

The Mortgage Process and Eligibility Requirements

The Mexican mortgaging process is very simple and is similar to the process in the United States. Because the closing process for a financed property may take slightly more time (approximately 30 days) than the closing process with cash, you should build this time into your schedule at the beginning of the process.

Your eligibility requirements will depend on the type of mortgage you are applying for. ConfiCasa Mortgage International offers several loan programs that are tailored to meet the needs of a variety of types of properties and buyers, including an exclusive loan program only available through ConfiCasa. While requirements for mortgage companies will vary on each case, here is list of ConfiCasa's general requirements to give an idea of your eligibility:

- Put a minimum of 20 percent down

- Be a U.S. or Canadian citizen or green card holder

- Meet a minimum credit score

- Require a minimum $100,000 loan

Some financing options require more than 20 percent down, depending on the purchase price, property, and borrower. Your interest rate and the type of loan you will qualify for will be largely determined by consideration of the following factors. These factors will vary depending on your mortgage company.

Your Credit Score

Most lenders will require you to meet a minimum FICO credit score to qualify for a loan. Your score is based on a number of factors, including how much revolving debt you have, what credit cards you currently have open, if you have paid your bills on time, if you have any liens on any property, and how long you have carried certain debt. You should always try to maximize your score before you apply for a loan. If you do not have an ideal score, you can easily improve it by doing the following:

> *Paying off your debt.* Paying off any revolving or unresolved debt before you apply for a loan can dramatically increase your chances of being approved by bumping up your credit score. Pay off the debt you have had the longest first. Student loan and some other kinds of debt are not seen as risky as credit card debt, so you should pay off high-risk debt first.

> *Using only a few lines of credit.* Having too many credit cards, used or unused, can weigh your score down significantly. Close any unused cards and minimize your use of existing

credit cards. Never exceed the limit on a card. Not only will credit card companies often allow you to exceed your limit for a hefty fee, but also it will show up on your credit score.

Making payments on time. It sounds simple enough, but it makes a world of difference. Any late payments will show up on your credit report and could damage your chances of receiving a loan.

The Loan-to-Value Ratio

A loan-to-value ratio is essentially an assessment of risk to the lender. It compares the amount of your loan to the value of the property, and takes into consideration your credit score, debt, and your income, among other factors. "The loan-to-value ratio is the percentage of the amount you are borrowing against the value of the property," Miller explained. For instance, if a buyer wants to borrow $150,000 for a property valued at $200,000, the loan-to-value ratio would be calculated by dividing the loan amount of $150,000 by the purchase price of $200,000. The loan-to-value ratio is the percentage of the amount you are borrowing against the value of the property. In this formula, the loan-to-value ratio percentage is 75 percent.

Typically, lenders like to see a loan-to-value ratio percentage under 80 percent. The lower your number, the less risk to the lender and the more likely your mortgage will get approved. Your credit score plays a role in determining this number, so working on paying down any debt will help increase your loan-to-value ratio. Additionally, "the purchase price, duration of the loan and region that your property is located also plays a role in the loan-to-value ratio," Miller said.

The Type of Property You Are Purchasing and How You Will Use it

Because condos, town homes, and single-family homes in resort and development communities are the most popular types of properties among foreign investors, mortgage companies are most often used to approve loans for these types of properties. The more well-known a development is, the more comfortable a mortgage company will be in providing a loan to you. However, this does not mean that you will not be approved for a single-family home in a lesser-known area of Mexico.

The type of loan you receive will also depend on how you plan to use your property. According to Matthew A. Miller, "There are two primary types of property usage for your Mexican property: vacation or second home and retirement property. If the property will be become your primary residence upon purchase, then it is considered a retirement property." If you plan to use your property for vacations or investment purposes and do not plan to live there year-round, it will be considered a vacation or second home.

Visit ConfiCasa Mortgage International to inquire about a Mexican loan at **www.conficasamortgageinternational.com**

How to Buy With Little Money Down

Mortgage lenders require a minimum of 20 percent down on Mexican properties. At first glance, it may seem like this is not a bargain, but consider the fact that although prices are steadily rising as purchasing property in Mexico becomes more and more popular, it is still possible to buy a nice home in Mexico for as little as $100,000 — and sometimes less. If your lender requires

20 percent down, all you would need to produce is $20,000. Compared to similar homes in the United States and other countries, a $20,000 down payment is very reasonable. The key is to look for a lower-value property in an up-and-coming area.

Aside from mortgaging a property, there are a variety of other options available to buyers interested in purchasing a Mexican property. Using home equity and an IRA account are two of the more common ways to finance, but additional methods can include using a reverse mortgage, purchasing with multiple investors, and even financing through the seller.

Using Your IRA to Finance

If you are purchasing property for investment only, it is possible and easy to finance using a real estate IRA. An IRA is a tax-free individual retirement account that can only be drawn from when you retire. People have used their IRAs to invest in a variety of things from real estate to start-up companies for decades.

Although not entirely common, setting up what is called a self-directed IRA will allow you to use funds from an existing IRA account to purchase real estate. The process involves finding a bank to grant you the loan and act as your trustee, similar to the process of establishing a *fideicomiso*. The bank then acts as your trustee, and you direct them to use your IRA account to invest in property. The bank, acting as the beneficiary, controls the property and collects all profits from any rental income. When you are eligible to collect your IRA funds, the trust is transferred to you, and you can sell the property and collect any profits from the sale.

Banks are not always willing to offer you these specialized services unless they involve a significant amount of money, and unless you pay with cash. You are not likely to get a self-directed IRA loan for a property worth, say, $100,000, simply because it does not benefit the bank to take on the risk and responsibility unless it is a high-end property. Also, if you do not have $100,000 in your IRA account, you would seek a mortgage company to essentially lend money to the IRA, which would then purchase your property. Mortgage lenders are hesitant about lending money to IRAs because of the complications in the process, so you would be most successful using your IRA account to purchase if you have the amount available and do not have to involve a lender.

Pensco Trust Company is one of a few dozen companies that offer self-directed IRA loans for real estate purchases. Visit their Web site to learn more at **www.penscotrust.com.**

Now that IRA accounts are protected by the government and FDIC-insured for up to $250,000, using an IRA to purchase investment property outside the country is becoming more popular. The downsides of using an IRA to finance a purchase are the inability to use your property for personal use, and the bank that grants you the loan has control of the property and collects any rental income. The upsides are the ability to use funds that would otherwise be unavailable to you to invest in property that will ultimately make you more money. You will also protect your money from the risk of losing money in other investments and potentially generate more income from the real estate investment than you would leaving your money in the IRA account.

It is, however, risky to use retirement money for a real estate purchase unless you have additional funds to use for living, medical, and emergency expenses. There is no guarantee you will make your money back on a real estate purchase or that you will be able to liquidate the money and use it quickly. It is best to use retirement funds only if you have additional funds tucked away for living expenses in your retirement years.

Using Home Equity to Finance

A home equity loan is a loan against the value of your primary home. It involves putting your house up as collateral for a line of credit and allows you to liquidate the equity in your home, which enables you to purchase property as well as many other things.

The positive aspects of a home equity line are the relatively low interest rates that are available, and the interest you will pay on the loan may be tax deductible. Because you are putting up your home as collateral, lenders are more willing to finance a home equity loan than other types of loans, as they can take possession should you default.

On the negative side, putting up your home for collateral is a significant risk. If you are unable to make payments — which will begin as soon as you are granted the loan — you risk losing your home.

PART IV

Mexican Living

CHAPTER 11

Life in Mexico

Deciding whether living in Mexico — either full- or part-time — is right for you will have a significant impact on if you purchase property in the country and where you do so. Like most every country, Mexico is richly diverse and offers a wide variety of lifestyles suitable for almost every need, want, budget, and expectation.

Researching the way of life in Mexico will give you a basic understanding of the culture, but the best way to do this is by experiencing it. Many people who are considering purchasing property visit Mexico several times before they commit to purchasing, traveling to different towns and talking to people, asking questions, and living the lifestyle for a short period of time to test it out. There is no better way to research the culture than experiencing it firsthand, which is why it is recommended to rent for a few months before committing to purchasing.

FAST FACTS ON MEXICO

Population: Nearing 112 million

Climate: Tropical and desert

Capital City: Mexico City

Structure: 31 states with 1 federal district

Religion: Mostly Roman Catholic

Languages: Spanish is the official language, but English is widely spoken

Government: Federal Republic

The hardest thing for many Americans or Canadians considering moving to Mexico to do is to adjust to a new culture and leave behind friends and family. But overall, Mexico is a warm and welcoming country, and its laid-back atmosphere, along with its affordable lifestyle, is what attracts many retirees and vacationers from all parts of the world.

Mexican Culture

Many people looking for property in Mexico naturally gravitate to a place that offers some of the comforts of home. If having American stores available to you and living amongst people similar to you is important, for instance, moving to a bigger city like Guadalajara might be wise because of access to stores like Costco Wholesale and McDonald's. There are many areas similar to Guadalajara like Los Cabos and Lake Chapala that are largely Americanized towns and offer a very different experience and culture than many other parts of Mexico.

Conversely, if you are looking for a more authentic location, a smaller, lesser-known beach town might be the way to go. If you are a natural adventurer and want a more rugged atmosphere, perhaps living in a small mountain town is ideal for you. It all depends on what is important to you and what kind of culture and lifestyle you would like to experience.

Like the United States and other countries, there are a variety of social norms and customs that many older generations adhere to, but younger generations are beginning to form new ones. This makes Mexico diverse and enables you as a foreigner to incorporate your own customs and social norms into the Mexican culture without feeling like too much of an outsider. In general, Mexican people are very warm, friendly, and willing to help.

This is, of course, contingent on how you treat the people of Mexico. Some Americans who do not take the time to understand the cultural and social norms of the country before spending time there often give off a bad vibe to the Mexican people by disrespecting them, unintentionally or not. For instance, Mexico is focused on the proper use of language, and one should use the formal word for "you" when speaking to someone who is an elder. Similarly, it is custom to use a more formal name when addressing someone and wait for that person to invite you to use his or her first name.

Mexico is mainly Roman Catholic, with a significant Protestant population, but it is religiously diverse. Society is structured around the family life, and families are often quite large in Mexico. Mexican families value each other greatly, and this hospitality often extends well beyond the immediate family. The structure of the immediate family is more traditional, with the father and husband considered the leader, and the mother and wife the caretaker of the home and children.

Holidays are a significant part of Mexican culture. Some of the more well known are *Cinco de Mayo* and the Mexican Day of the Dead, along with Mexican Independence Day. Many holidays are celebrated with elaborate street fairs, fireworks, dancing, food, and music. The Day of the Dead is celebrated by honoring those who have passed; this is done by visiting the gravesites and bringing flowers and gifts.

Additionally, art and handmade crafts are an important part of Mexican culture, as is music. Crafts like jewelry, furniture, baskets, dolls, masks, sculptures, and figurines are abundant. Many Americans who purchase property in Mexico find beautiful handcrafted items indigenous to the local culture that they collect and use to furnish and decorate their Mexican homes.

Etiquette

The rules of etiquette in Mexico focus on manners and politeness. While many of these etiquette rules may seem obvious, it is important to be aware of them, particularly if you plan to live in community of mostly Mexican nationals. The following are some basic rules of etiquette:

1. Always address others as "Senor," "Senorita," or by their last name until you are invited to use their first name.

2. If you are invited into someone's home ahead of time, bring a small gift like candy or flowers. Stay away from marigolds, which are associated with death; red flowers are also sometimes considered bad luck.

3. Churches and religious institutions should be respected. When entering a religious facility of any kind, remove your hat — and if you have a cell phone, be sure to turn it off.

4. If you are presented with a gift, open it immediately and express your appreciation and gratitude.

5. If you are meeting someone for the first time, shake his or her hand politely. Only when you know someone well is it custom to kiss them on the cheek.

6. If you are invited to someone's house for dinner, finish your meal to express your gratitude for the food.

6. Similarly, keep your hands visible when you share a meal with a Mexican national, and use the same rules of eating etiquette you would in the United States: Place your utensils across your plate, with prongs facing to the right when you are finished eating.

7. Say *salud* ("bless you") when someone sneezes.

8. Even if you cannot speak Spanish well, use it instead of English when you can. Assuming a Mexican should know English instead of attempting to use their native language could be considered rude.

9. Greet and acknowledge everyone you come into contact with, including workers, waitresses, store owners, and even people on the streets.

10. Expect things to happen at a slower pace. People often arrive late for events and meetings; in fact, in some areas of Mexico, it is considered rude to arrive on time.

Is it equally important to learn the specific rules of etiquette for your particular area of Mexico. There may be rules and nuances you cannot discover until you ask around.

Language

The official language of Mexico is Spanish, but English is widely spoken, particularly in the more Americanized areas of the country, like Puerto Vallarta and Los Cabos. This does not mean that you should not take the time to learn basic Spanish terminology, however, as it will help you greatly. You should always attempt to speak to a Mexican national in Spanish as opposed to English. It is considered rude to assume that someone should know your language, especially if you are not attempting to use the native language.

Shopping & Food

Shopping for food, clothes, and household goods is more than a chore for most Mexicans; it is a social activity. Street markets are abundant in Mexico, as are roadside stands for food. Buying the foods that are abundant in Mexico, like tortillas, beans, tomatoes, and other fruits and vegetables native to your particular area will be the least expensive. If you are looking for novelty items, prepare to pay a significantly higher price as these items may be imported. If you wish to purchase high quality meats, it is wise, depending on where you live, to do so at an American store, like Costco, or a high-quality butcher.

The majority of Mexican food is centered on ingredients, including beans, vegetables, meats, fruits, and corn. Some of the best tortillas and Mexican dishes can be found at roadside taco and food stands, and in small, authentic restaurants. Vegetables and fruits at these roadside stands are also very inexpensive, but it wise to wash everything you can before eating it. Although the water is safe to drink and use for cooking in many areas of Mexico, it is still questionable for foreigners in some areas of the country, so it is wise to use filtered or bottled water even to clean food.

Shopping in neighborhood markets and at roadside stands is the cheapest way to purchase food; bigger grocery stores have higher prices.

Everyday Living Expenses

Many people move to Mexico because of the very low cost of living. There is a bit of a misconception over how much it actually costs to live in Mexico, and the truth is that this depends on what kind of lifestyle you want to lead. If you want to live in an exclusive gated community in Los Cabos, visit private medical doctors, and hire a live-in maid, you can expect to have monthly expenses similar to your expenses in the United States or Canada.

If you are looking to live a bit more frugally, it is possible to sustain yourself on as little as $1,000 a month or less, including rent or a mortgage payment, depending on where you live, how you live, and your monthly mortgage payment. If you plan on renting — and, again, this depends significantly on which part of Mexico you plan to rent in — you can easily find a nice home for $200-$300 a month in rent, and maybe even less.

Electricity and Power

If you do not use air conditioning and heat, your electricity bill will be fairly inexpensive, even though the cost of energy can be more expensive in Mexico than the United States and Canada. Given that the average temperature is 70-80 degrees in many areas of Mexico throughout the year, you will likely use much less electricity to heat and cool your home than you would in most areas of the United States and Canada.

Phones, Internet, and Television

Phone service will cost you around $20 to $25 per month, as will Internet access. If you want broadband service, you can expect to pay more. Mexico has many Internet cafes, and for about $1 or $2 an hour, you can access the Internet.

Phone service in Mexico often includes only a limited amount of long-distance calls, if any. Some foreigners use calling cards instead of a Mexican phone service provider or their carrier in their home country. Some phone companies based in the United States and Canada offer international plans, and this may be cheaper than paying for long-distance service in Mexico.

There is also the option of an internet phone service like Dialpad/ Yahoo! Voice (**www.dialpad.com**) and Skype (**www.skype.com**), a service that allows you to make free calls using the internet.

Unless you upgrade to a more advanced cable television package or live in an area that receives English-speaking channels, your television service will include basic Spanish language channels. Some foreigners invest in satellite television for specialized channels that are not accessible on basic Mexican television.

Maid Service

Enlisting the services of a maid is very common in Mexico, considering the average cost is so low compared to the cost of this service in the United States and Canada. Maid services average about $1 to $3 per hour or a couple hundred dollars a month, depending on where you live and what kind of services you expect. Many households even employ a live-in maid to take care of laundry, cooking, cleaning, and other household chores. This is common among wealthier Mexican families and foreigners.

Food

Excluding high-end restaurants in touristy areas of Mexico, restaurant meals are very cheap. A full-course meal can cost you as little as $4 or $5 in some restaurants in more rural and less touristy areas of Mexico. If you are planning to live in places like Puerto Vallarta or Los Cabos, prepare to pay significantly more than this for a restaurant meal. Below is a sample list of average costs for select food items in Mexico to give you an idea of expenses. Costs greatly depend on geographical location and availability; costs may vary depending on if you purchase in a supermarket or a roadside stand.

Rice: 30 cents a pound
Oranges: 20 cents a pound
Apples: 50-60 cents a pound
Hamburger Meat: $1.50 a pound
Milk: $1.80 a gallon
Bottle of Wine: $4 to $5

Medical Care

Mexico offers excellent medical care in some areas for much less than the cost of medical care in the Unites States in particular. Costs for dentist visits, surgeries, doctor's visits, and prescriptions are drastically less expensive. A doctor's office visit can cost as little as $15 in some areas, and a teeth cleaning at a local clinic can cost somewhere in the range of $50 to $80. Advanced dental work that would cost upward of $8,000 in the United States can run you under $2,000 in Mexico at some clinics. Prescription drugs that would normally cost you hundreds of dollars a month can often be purchased in the generic form in Mexico for $15 or $20. You may need to seek permission from your doctor in your home country to fill prescriptions in Mexico.

As far as medical insurance, if you are a tourist, you will likely be covered under your policy at home while you are in Mexico. If you are living in Mexico permanently or part-time, you will have to get a policy through an insurance company that offers international health insurance policies. Some medical centers and hospitals also offer insurance that is specific to that center. If you are a legal resident of Mexico, you may be entitled to the Mexican Social Security Insurance, which requires a yearly payment and covers a variety of medical and dental services and procedures.

Of course, you must be cautious about which medical facilities you choose for services and treatment. Even though medical care options are increasing drastically in Mexico, you should still research a facility before you receive care or treatment. Better yet, ask your neighbors and the locals for a recommendation. Despite advancements in health care in Mexico, there are still certain instances where a medical facility in your home country can better treat your condition.

Safety

The topic of crime and the Mexican drug cartels have come up more in recent months as the issues gain more attention in the global media. Although violence and crime are increasing in some areas of Mexico because of the drug cartels, these are isolated areas, hundreds of miles away from the majority of locations you would consider purchasing in. "Just because they are fighting over turf in Tijuana does not means that fighting is spilling over to [areas like] Los Cabos," Chris Snell explained. "Just imagine if you did not like the crime rate in New York, so you decided to move to Tennessee, which is 1,000 miles away." One of the biggest misconceptions is that the drug wars are taking over Mexico.

As in any other country, taking basic precautionary steps to protect yourself and your home will help reduce the chances that theft or crime will affect you. When you are out in town, especially in a crowded area, do not place your wallet in your back pocket. Keep a purse or back pack in front of you to avoid theft. Crime rates are very low in many areas of Mexico, but locking your house every time you leave and installing an alarm system is a good idea. If you are planning on being at your Mexican home only a few months a year, enlist a property manager or a friend to manage your property when you are away to avoid theft and damage.

Banking

Banking is easy to handle in Mexico and does not require much of a disruption from your system at home. Mexico has a variety of international banks, and your bank at home may even have an affiliate in Mexico, which makes it very easy to manage your finances. If your bank does not offer international services, you can set up an account with a Mexican or an international bank that will enable you to deposit checks from the United States or Canada.

Depending on the value of the peso, it could be wise to keep your bank accounts in the United States and withdraw from these once a month or so to pay for expenses. Because the value of the peso fluctuates frequently, most foreigners living in Mexico stick to a U.S. bank. As with many other aspects of moving to Mexico as a foreigner, banking services are improving in Mexico.

Mexican Visas and Immigration Guidelines

Mexico has a variety of immigration guidelines and classifications. As a foreigner purchasing property and spending time in Mexico, you will most likely fall into one of three categories.

FMT

The FMT is a tourist visa and is intended for those who are staying in Mexico a short amount of time to vacation. It can be granted for up to six months, but it usually granted for no longer than

90 days because it is intended for short-term stay. The visa can be renewed every time you come back to Mexico.

FM3

An FM3 is a temporary residential visa that allows you to be in the country temporarily or spend part of the year in Mexico. It is intended for people who wish to retain their citizenship in their home country but acquire certain rights and a residency in Mexico.

It is referred to a *no inmigrante* (non-immigrant) visa, and to meet these requirements, you must prove an income, even if you own property. Most people who purchase property for vacation or second-home purchases as opposed to retirement and primary residences aim to get an FM3 visa, which also allows you to have a car registered in Mexico. The FM3 will be valid for one year and can be renewed several times.

FM2

An FM2 is an immigration visa intended for those who wish to ultimately make Mexico their permanent residence. It has more stringent requirements than an FM3 because you may apply for an FM3, the non-immigrant visa, after five years of meeting FM2 requirements. The status is deemed *inmigrante* ("immigrant") and carries certain rights that mirror those of a Mexican national, excluding the right to vote.

CONCLUSION

Purchasing property in Mexico has been popular for decades, but only with the recently amended laws and additional regulations can your investment be truly protected. The Mexican government encourages foreigners to purchase property in their beautiful country and have instituted a number of processes and regulations that enable foreigners to buy with more ease and peace of mind than ever before.

The process of purchasing has made headway and will continue to do so in the future. The Mexican government continues to invest millions of dollars into its tourism industry to attract foreigners to the country and to build up the country's real estate to make it readily available for purchase. More and more foreigners are tapping into the enormous potential investment opportunities in Mexico, and developers, real estate agents, banks, and the government are all working to meet the increasing demands of affordable homes in Mexico.

For you, this means options. More financing, location, and property options means more control on your end, and it makes it much easier to find your ideal property and negotiate a deal that works best for you. Particularly in a buyer's market, when developers and sellers are very eager to unload their properties at discounted prices, the real estate world is your oyster. Because of the unique position the Mexican market is in right now — and will probably stay in for just a short while — you have a great opportunity to invest.

In reality, Mexico is a wonderful, safe, thriving country, and purchasing property for an investment, a second home, or vacation purposes is easier than ever. The sun, surf, and sand are only part of the draw; the people, the culture, the atmosphere, and now the lure of affordable, luxurious real estate on some of the most beautiful land in the world are drawing flocks of people from all corners of the globe to get their little piece of heaven. Musician James Taylor said it best when he sang, "Oh, Mexico sounds so simple. I just got to go."

APPENDIX

Real Estate Terms
You Need to Know

AMPI: *La Asociación Mexicana de Profesionales Inmobiliarios* (Association of Mexican Real Estate Professionals). AMPI ensures real estate agents are qualified and professional.

Avalúo: An appraisal of the land.

Beneficiary: A person who receives or is named to receive the benefits in terms of money, goods, real estate, or other assets.

Capital: Start-up money in the form of cash to invest in a project.

Capital Gain: The amount of money you gain from the sale of a property, after you have paid back any lenders and fees.

Capital Gains Tax: Tax you are required to pay on the gains you make from selling a secondary residence property.

Caveat Emptor: Translates to "buyer beware;" the buyer is responsible for ensuring a purchase is in his or her best interest.

Certificate of No Encumbrances: A certificate that ensures the property has no liens against it.

Certificate of No Tax Liability: A certificate that ensures there is no tax owed on the property.

Clear Title: A title to a property that indicates the property has no liens, debts, defaults, or legal issues.

Closing: The final step in the purchasing process when the final contract — The Purchase and Sales Agreement — is signed, the title is transferred to the buyer, and the balance of the sale is transferred to the seller.

Closing Costs: All costs related to closing a real estate transaction. In Mexico, these include all agents' and attorney's fees, permit fees, appraisal fees, acquisition taxes, *notario* fees, and trust fees, among others.

Comparative Market Analysis (CMA): A report that compares similar properties and their sales prices in a given geographical area.

Commercial Property: Property that someone intends to use for commercial purposes, such as a retail store, hotel, or restaurant.

Condominium: A type of property that is individually owned but part of a larger development in which everyone in the development commonly owns some areas.

Construction Loan: A specific type of loan granted in various payments throughout the construction process to fund construction of a property.

Cooperative: Referred to as "co-op;" this type of property is owned by shareholders, who own a certain amount of shares of the property and own the right to reside in a single unit (usually an apartment unit).

Cost-Plus Contract: A type of contract that dictates you pay the builder for all construction costs plus an additional percentage.

Counteroffer: An offer made in response to a previous offer.

Deed: A document that officially assigns ownership of a property to a buyer.

Developer: A person who uses capital to build a property, usually a community or subdivision, and then sells part or all of that property for a profit.

Development: A self-sustaining community of homes usually developed and run by a developer, often including individual units and common areas.

Due Diligence: The research process a potential buyer and his or her mortgager should take to ensure a property is free of any defects and is being presented accurately by the seller.

Earnest Money Deposit: Funds a buyer will deposit to a secure third party to initiate the purchasing process and ensure the seller that the buyer is serious about purchasing. Earnest money deposits are usually forfeited if the buyer defaults.

Ejido: Communal land established by the Mexican government for use by peasants who petitioned to use the land.

Ejiditario: A person who lives on *ejidal* property.

Equity: The value of a property less anything owed on the property. The amount of equity available in your home will determine how much you can take out for a home equity loan.

Escritura publica: The public deed to a property. This must be obtained before a property can be transferred to a new owner.

Escrow: An account held by a third party to which funds are deposited and held while the terms of a contract are defined and met.

FDIC: Stands for Federal Deposit Insurance Corporation, an independent government agency that provides insurance to deposits made to banks.

Fideicomiso: A trust with a Mexican national bank established when a foreigner wants to purchase property within 30 miles of the coast and 60 miles from any international border.

Fixed-Cost Contract: A contract that states the cost of a service will remain the same throughout the service.

Foreigner: Any person who does not have Mexican citizenship. Foreigners may become Mexican citizens through nationalization.

Gringo: Spanish word used to describe Americans, or any Caucasian person.

Homeowner's Association (HOA): An entity or corporation established to run a development and handle all the legal, development, sales, and management issues of the development.

Immigrante: Immigrant

IVA Tax: *Impuesto al Valor Agregado.* This is a sales tax

Lien: A legal hold over a property. This may come in the form of taxes owed, funds owed on a mortgage, or from any other debt owed.

Lender: Any party that supplies funds in the form of a loan to another party.

Loan: Amount borrowed from a third party, most often repayable with interest over a set period of time.

Loan-to-Value Ratio: The ratio of the amount lent to the borrower and the value of the property being purchased.

Mexican National: According to the Mexican Constitution, nationals include all persons born of Mexican parents, naturalized foreigners, and foreigners who have children born in Mexico, unless they preserve their nationality by proper declaration.

Mortgage: A loan obtained from a third party to purchase real estate.

Multiple Listing Service (MLS): An online service that lists properties being sold to a variety of brokers.

National Association of Realtors (NAR): A national organization of qualified and professional real estate agents.

Notario Publico: Notary public; a person appointed by the Mexican government who is an attorney with five years of experience.

No Inmigrante: Non-immigrant

Normas Oficiales Mexicana (NOM): National standards that regulate timesharing and provide protection to timeshare buyers and investors.

Perito Valuador: An official appraiser.

Preliminary Title Report: A document detailing the history of a title to a property.

Promissory Agreement: The first of two to three contracts you will sign essentially promises you will purchase a property.

Purchase-Sales Agreement: The final of two to three contracts you will sign that defines the sale of the property.

Registro Nacional de Inversiones Extranjeras **(RNIE):** The National Foreign Investment Registry

Restricted Zone: Any property located within 30 miles of the coast and 60 miles from any international border. Also sometimes referred to as the foreign zone or the prohibited zone.

Single-Family Home: A detached home that is not part of any other structure.

Secretaría de Relaciones Exteriores **(SRE):** The Secretary of External Relations. This government organization is in charge of visas, immigration, and citizenship.

Transfer Tax: Also called the acquisitions tax; is paid by the buyer and is currently around 2 percent of the total value of the property.

Timeshare: A type of ownership in which the owner does not own the property but rather the rights to use the property during designated time periods throughout the year.

Title: A document that demonstrates ownership of a property.

Title Search: The process of researching the history of a title to determine any defects.

Title Insurance: Insurance that protects against certain defaults in a property's title.

Unimproved Land: Land that is absent of development in the sense of electricity, water supply, and gas lines and other necessities. Sometimes referred to as raw land.

BIBLIOGRAPHY

Haden, Jeff, *The Complete Dictionary of Real Estate Terms Explained Simply: What Smart Investors Need to Know*, Florida: Atlantic Publishing Company, 2007.

Kerr, Robert Joseph. *A Handbook of Mexican Law: Being an Abridgement of the Principal Mexican Codes*. Chicago: Pan American Law Book Company, 1909.

"The Foreign Investment Law," 1993. Official Gazette of the Federation. April 27, 2009.

Miller, Matthew A., "Do I Need to Obtain Title Insurance For The Purchase of My Mexico Real Estate?" 2009, **www.conficasamortgageinternational.com/faqs/mexico+mortgage+loan.php#faq6**.

Miller, Matthew A., "What Product Features Should Be Considered When Seeking a Mexico Mortgage Loan?" 2009, **www.conficasamortgage international.com/faqs/mexico+mortgage+loan.php**.

Miller, Matthew A. "What Are the Benefits in Obtaining Mexico Mortgage Financing for My Mexico Dream Home?" 2009, **www.conficasamortgage international.com/faqs/mexico+mortgage+loan.php**.

Miller, Matthew A. "Clarifying Many Misconceptions," 2009, **www.conficasamortgageinternational.com/financing-101/mexico+mortgage+loan.php#misconceptions**.

Neil, Linda, "Buying Real Estate in Mexico," 2004, **www.lindaneil.com/articles/buyingrealestatemexico.pdf**.

Neil, Linda, "Protecting Your Home — Selecting the Property Manager," 2004, **www.lindaneil.com/articles/selectingpropertymanager.pdf**.

Neil, Linda, "Agency and the Real Estate Agent," 2004, **www.lindaneil.com/articles/agencyprofessionalism.pdf**.

Neil, Linda. "Buying Real Estate in Coastal or Border Areas," 2004,
www.lindaneil.com/articles/buyingrealestateinmexicancoastalareas.pdf.

Neil, Linda. "Purchasing Your Dream Home in Mexico," 2004,
www.lindaneil.com/articles/dreamhomeinmexico.pdf.

Neil, Linda, "The Legal Aspects of Living in a Condominium," 2004,
www.lindaneil.com/articles/condolivingmexico.pdf.

Niemi, Jeff, "Before You Begin Construction," 2005,
www.bajabeachinvestments.com/Home_Building_Tips/page_806847.html.

Tremblay, Jason, "Is Timeshare An Investment Property?" 2008,
www.thetimeshareauthority.com/2008/09/03/is-timeshare-an-investment-property/

AUTHOR BIOGRAPHY

Photo by Elizabeth Sagarin

Jackie Bondanza is a developmental book editor and freelance writer. She has written on real estate, education, entertainment, travel, health, and lifestyle for iVillage, MSN, *Online Degrees* Magazine, *Hemispheres* Magazine, *Southern California Senior Life*, *Northridge* Magazine, and *College Bound Teen* Magazine. She has a master's degree in journalism and has written copy for both television and radio. She has also appeared as an education and lifestyle consultant for a variety of national television programs.

As a developmental editor, Bondanza works with authors to develop books ranging in genre from historical nonfiction and reference to pop culture and literature. In addition to her editorial work, Jackie writes a blog on international aid issues for Globalhood, an international consultancy firm, and she also leads workshops for homeless writers around the country. She currently lives in New York City with her husband and dog and looks forward owning a home in Mexico in the near future. Visit her at **www. JackieBondanza.com**.

INDEX